Black Dog Zen

THE WISDOM IN
SHORT STORIES & PERCEPTION

VOLUME 1
FINDING YOUR SUNSPOT

Laura A. Kitch

Black Dog Zen

THE WISDOM
IN SHORT STORIES & PERCEPTION

Laura A. Kitch

Black Dog Zen

The Wisdom in Short Stories & Perception

by Laura A. Kitch

ISBN-13:

978-1-955688-00-0 (pbk)

MindfulCalm Press

* * *

Disclaimer:

 Many of the stories included in this handbook have been told numerous times, in various forms, through many years. Where I could locate an original author, that person has been identified. In most cases these stories have been altered so many times and told in so many forms the original source is difficult to clarify. Many of these stories can be easily found in books, on television, in movies, on the Internet and in many other forums. Some are personal anecdotes or creative adaptations of experiences shared with me. Others are imagined stories. None are direct accounts of any specific individual, if not specifically mentioned, and are to be seen as amalgamations of us all rather than specific to any individual. It is my hope that these stories and others like them continue to encourage us to be compassionate and connected explorers.

Dedication

For Alexandra & James

Always stay curious, kind and hard-working.

Find your sunspot, carry it with you wherever you go,

and spread your light.

"A good story captures your attention.

A better story makes you pause to consider something

differently or learn something new.

A great story inspires you to challenge yourself, to

expand beyond an established expectation and to risk

shifting a position previously held."

— LK

Introduction

Welcome to *Black Dog Zen, Finding Your Sunspot*, a collection of stories designed to provide easy-to-find motivational stories for any situation. The stories included in *Black Dog Zen* are inspirational in spirit and offer life lessons for contemplation and discussion. This book is intended as a source for personal enjoyment, to be shared as a gift, or used as a teaching/presentation tool. The more we share ideas and viewpoints, the better connected we become to our self, others and our environment.

The black dog in *Black Dog Zen*, is a real dog named Jack. Jack is an old guy now but through his years of living with my family we have all come to appreciate the wisdom of his ways. The last story in the categories section, "Find Your Sunspot," is a great example of Jack's teachings. Like the stories in this book, his teachings are simple in observation but profound in meaning, if you decide to dig in (dog humor). That is one commonality among short stories, koans, parables, and tales of fairies and folk. They allow us to construct our own interpretations and assign meaning to a communal message. There is no forced obligation to identify importance, just an invitation.

I developed a tradition of sharing stories in an unexpected way. It was a blunder resulting from nerves that started it. I was a newly certified yoga instructor and was given an impromptu opportunity to teach a yoga class at the studio where I often practiced yoga. The teacher had an emergency. I was invited to fill in for her.

I had no time to prepare (I like to prepare). In my corporate career I regularly presented to executives and large crowds, but the idea of leading a class of peers dressed in stretchy pants and expectations, with no preparation, was daunting. I felt my throat closing as I readied to speak and when I stood in front of the sea of yoga mats and glaring stares — I froze. Words wouldn't come out and panic mixed with jumbled yoga positions in my brain. Did anyone want to buy a global solution for their computing software environment? I wondered.

I felt judgment from the crowd and became defensive instead of open. I tried to stop worrying but that only made things worse. I took a deep breath to force myself to begin and without my conscious involvement I heard my voice fill the room and tell the class about . . . *Kinky Boots*? Where was this coming from? I had seen the show a few months earlier and hadn't thought much about it since, as far as I knew. The whole story is great, but I will just tell you the specific line that came to me that day, "Promise to change your mind about someone today." I loved the line when I heard it but I hadn't thought about it since. It must have been buried in my mind.

I offered the same consideration to my self and to the class, "Let's choose to change our minds about someone today." It opened the opportunity for a different outcome to occur. The shift was palpable and I felt that most of us did let go of our expectations enough to change our minds. At least I did and that changed everything. Those glaring eyes appeared to soften and felt welcoming instead interrogating, to me. I chose to see the beautiful people before me as eager instead of criticizing. The shift of how I decided to interpret the experience made the outcome completely different. Probably they shifted as well but the only piece that really and truly will affect change in our own life is how we choose to perceive and act in our experiences.

That experience impacted me so deeply that I started a tradition of sharing a story to open every yoga class I guide. That was a long time ago. This practice has changed my life. The insights, laughter, wisdom, knowledge and love shared while connecting through trading stories is unlike any other communication exchange I know. It is an open and friendly way of sharing and discovering new perspectives and creating better understanding about different ways of thinking.

A beautiful truth about stories unfolded before my eyes; stories shared are eternal and ever evolving. People started coming to class, in part at least, to hear the story of the day and many asked for copies of the stories. They were taking the stories home with them to be shared in new communities. Numerous people told me how the stories had become part of their own lives and had and changed ways they communicated with others. The examples of how people used the stories in their own lives energized me.

One yoga practitioner was a doctor. She developed a routine of inviting people to gather ten minutes before rounds to hear a motivating story. A nurse in that group set up an email chain for anyone who wanted to hear the story but couldn't attend the gathering. This doctor explained to me how the stories spread exponentially. The caregivers would share the stories with their patients, who would share them with visitors, and both shared the stories with colleagues and at home.

In addition, many yoga attendees told me how the stories had become expected at their family dinners and had helped to open numerous conversations that may have been avoided without the easy introduction a neutral story offered. Others gave the stories to celebrate events like weddings, new baby's, graduations, birthdays, etc. They also shared stories with people facing struggles like illness, divorce, loss, or depression. Stories provide additional intimacy in a gesture.

People seem to like giving stories as gifts or to create a theme for a gift. The final story in this book, "The Gift of the Raspberry," is a story that exhibits the beauty and power of this custom. So many people have expressed to me how sharing stories helped to change their relationships and conversations. I hope you will try it. Experience the circle of generosity and connection you receive when sharing stories.

Grateful Appreciation

I am grateful for all of the people who have shared stories with me. I send a special appreciation to my family for being the heart of my inspiration. I thank my mother for reading endless versions of my writing, for being my constant teacher in life, and always cheering me on. To Mark, I am grateful for all of the wonderful aspects of life we built together and the lessons we have shared. Thank you for providing for our family for many years. Alexandra and James, I am honored to be your mother. You amaze me more each day as you continue to grow and mature into ever-more incredible people. Thank you for embodying love and challenging me to stretch and grow each and every day. BYOS!

My deep appreciation goes out to all of those friends who took time to read this book in different phases and offered their sound advice. I celebrate all of the yogis and friends who have inspired this book and offered me many wonderful stories of their own. Thank you for teaching me just how special the tradition of story-sharing is! All are a huge part of this book and the ones to follow.

Let's spread the stories!

Table of Contents

I. Know Who You Are

"Who are YOU?" said the Caterpillar.

This was not an encouraging opening for a conversation. Alice replied, rather shyly, "I-I hardly know, sir, just at present — at least I know who I WAS when I got up this morning, but I think I must have been changed several times since then."

— Alice In Wonderland, *by Lewis Carroll*

Who are you? At first, you might be inclined to laugh at Alice's response to Caterpillar's question but after further thought you might realize it is challenging to describe who you are. Are you your actions, your roles, your achievements, your body, your thoughts? Something else? You will also realize that you are different from the person you once were. Certainly you are not the same now as you were at five or six years old. Are you? Perhaps something dramatic even happened to you this morning that has already influenced the way you are being today? There are countless ways that we change our "self" over time, even from moment to moment. But what makes the "who" in "you"?

Story 1

The Eagle Who Thought
She Was a Chicken

Adaptation. Original author unknown,
some version has been attributed to Anthony de Mello.

High up on a mountainside there was an eagle's nest. The eagle's nest contained four large eagle eggs. One day an earthquake rocked the mountain, shaking the nest and causing one of the eggs to roll down the mountain into a chicken coop that was located in the valley below. The chickens saw the egg and ignored it except for one mother chicken that decided to protect that egg just as she would her very own.

She kept the eagle egg warm just as she did her own eggs. When the day came that the large egg cracked and the eagle was born, the hen continued to care for the eagle as one of her own babies. She cared for the eagle just as she did her own young. She did all that she knew for the eagle but of course all she knew was how to be a chicken and so, the eagle was raised as a chicken and not the eagle she was.

Every day, the eagle pecked at the seeds scattered across the dirt with her fellow chickens, but she was always hungry for more. She would look up into the blue sky and feel a stirring in her belly and when an eagle would fly overhead she would say to her chicken family, "I would like to fly with them."

"Well, you *can't* fly for you are a chicken and chickens do not fly!" The other chickens clucked. They had no desire to fly and were perfectly happy waddling along the ground pecking at the seeds scattered for them to eat.

The eagle loved her home and family, but her spirit cried out for the blue sky and mountaintops. Her heart wanted to soar, and her belly felt empty feeding it only corn kernels. "Oh, I wish I could soar like those birds."

The chickens would mock and laugh at her reminding her, "You are a chicken and chickens do not soar."

The eagle stared to the sky watching a family of eagles fly above while the others were satisfied pecking at the dirt. Little did she know it was her biological family she was observing.

After some time, she wearied of being mocked and told it couldn't be done, so she kept quiet and pecked at the dirt along with the others trying to convince herself to behave more like, and desire as, a chicken should.

And so, the story goes . . . the eagle learned to believe that she was a chicken. After enough times of being told she was a foolish dreamer, the eagle had stopped imagining beyond her coop and settled to live her life like as a chicken.

After a long life living as a chicken, the eagle died . . . a chicken!

Thought:

If you act like a chicken you will live your life as a chicken and die a chicken. Don't peck if your desire is to *soar!* Follow the instincts of your spirit, the inner knowing that guides you when you listen for it rather adhering to restricting expectations. We are all chickens and eagles in life. Sometimes we are more able to find the courage to stand for our truth and take bold action while other times we step to the side and allow, if not support, outcomes that are not sincere for us. At times we spread our wings and soar like an eagle and other times we bow our heads and peck at the ground, acting like chickens while we ignore our truth. At any point we are able to change our behavior and create a new way of showing up in our lives.

Inquiry:

1. How connected to your intuition are you? Do you use your instincts in decisions you make?

2. How often do you find conflict between what you feel versus what you do?

3. Is there something you still want to be that you haven't tried becoming yet?

4. Do you consider yourself courageous? How could being brave change your life?

5. Are you living as a chicken or an eagle? Which do you choose to be?

Story 2

The Struggle of a Butterfly

*Adaptation from a story by unknown author, though a
version was sighted on Paulo Coelho's website and attributed
to a submission made by Sonaira D'Avila.*

One day, a little boy found an incredibly interesting
caterpillar and he brought it home to show his mother. He
asked if he could keep the caterpillar. His mother said that he
could for a while, if he took good care of it and set it up with
the right environment and food. Then, he would have to let it
go back into nature. The boy did just that, and soon he noticed
his caterpillar doing something strange. The mother explained
that the caterpillar had started to build a cocoon.

The boy watched closely each day as the caterpillar
completely enclosed itself in its cocoon. He waited and watched
anxiously for the caterpillar to re-emerge as a butterfly, as his

NNP2

mother had explained would happen next. After a few days, it started to happen. The butterfly made a small hole in the cocoon and was working to emerge.

The boy watched as days passed with the butterfly struggling to get out of the cocoon but making what appeared to be little progress. He began to worry that the butterfly was struggling too much and was becoming weak. The boy decided to help the butterfly. He found a pair of scissors and gently cut the space where the fat bellied butterfly was beginning to emerge. When the hole was large enough the butterfly escaped easily but it looked odd. It had a swollen body and shriveled wings.

The boy continued to care for the butterfly, expecting that the wings would grow large enough to support its body, which he thought would contract in time. That never happened. The butterfly spent the rest of its life crawling around with its swollen body and shriveled wings and was never able to fly.

In his intention of kindness, the boy didn't realize that the restricting cocoon and the struggle required for the butterfly to get through the tiny opening were nature's way of forcing fluid from the body of the butterfly to its wings so that it would be ready for flight once it achieved freedom. The struggle was the only way to prepare for the freedom of flight to come.

Thought:

We are of changing form and resilience, shaped and strengthened by the challenges we endure in life. Perhaps, the struggles we face are exactly what we need to become stronger and evolve into our new form. Resistance builds strength in muscle and spirit to overcome the obstacles we encounter and equips us with the power to endure. Without the experiential knowledge and fortitude derived from hard work and perseverance we wouldn't have the strength and wisdom we need to *fly*.

Inquiry:

1. Do you embrace challenges as progress toward improvement?
2. Can you identify a difficult experience that aided your evolution into a healthier form?
3. How did the struggle strengthen you?
4. Do you consider yourself beautiful in your current form?
5. Are you patient? Do you often want to rush a process you are in?
6. Do you value transformation? How would you like to see yourself transform?

Story 3

The Man, the Boy, and the Donkey

Aesop. (Sixth century B.C.) Fables.

A man and his son were walking their donkey to market As they walked by its side a countryman passed them and commented,

"You fools! What is a donkey for if not to ride upon?"

So the man put the boy on the donkey and they went on their way.

But soon they passed a group of men, one who said: "See that lazy youngster who lets his father walk as he rides."

So the man ordered the boy get off and, got on himself. But they hadn't gone far when they passed two women one of whom said to the other: "Shame on that lazy lout to let his poor little son trudge along."

Well, the man didn't know what to do, but at last he took his boy up before him on the donkey. By this time they had come to the town, and the passers-by began to jeer and point at them. The man stopped and asked what they were scoffing at. The men said: "Aren't you ashamed of yourself for overloading that donkey of yours — you and your hulking son?"

The man and the boy got off and tried to think of what to do. They thought and they thought, till at last they cut down a pole, tied the donkey's feet to it, and raised the pole and the donkey to their shoulders.

They went along amid the laughter of all who met them until they came to the Market Bridge, where the donkey, getting one of his feet loose, kicked out and caused the boy to drop his end of the pole. In the struggle the donkey fell over the bridge, and his forefeet being tied he was drowned.

"That will teach you," said an old man who had followed them:

"Please All and You Will Please None!"

Thought:

You can't please everyone, so don't waste time trying to. Listen to your own wisdom to guide your actions while remaining open to learn. Do not perceive judgment as wisdom. If you build your choices on the judgments of others your will never trust your own knowledge. Observe to learn but remember that other people's opinions are only for contemplation not obedience. Also . . .

If you try to please everyone you may as well kiss your ass good-bye!

Inquiry:

1. Can you recall a situation that you allowed yourself to be swayed by other's opinions away from your own? Was it for good result? Looking back, would you change your behavior?

2. Why do you think people forgo their own wisdom and defer to another's opinion? Is it insecurity? A desire to please? Being open? Being Agreeable? Being irresponsible?

3. What are the perceived benefits to being accommodating to external judgment?

4. Do you pause long enough to know your own answers in situations before following another's decision or instruction?

5. Do you feel comfortable standing up to do what you think is right?

6. What do you know for certain?

Story 4

The New King

— LK

There once was a tyrant who ruled a kingdom. He was cruel and threatening to all.

He ruled for only a few years, ruining the beauty and wealth of the kingdom in that short time. The villagers were left starved for healthy food and void of all resources or material goods because the king had taken all the valuables for himself. Even the king's protectors had been treated with such harshness they'd become shells of the strong defenders they'd once been.

Then the king died and his son took position as the new king.

Though the kingdom was pleased that their scornful ruler was gone, they doubted that his son would be able to lead them successfully. The son had been born with extreme facial deformities and, in an effort born from maternal protection, the Queen had demanded all mirrors be removed from the kingdom to prevent her son from ever seeing his reflection, so he was unaware of his different appearance.

The son grew into adulthood never knowing of his physical differences. Eventually, none saw him by his physical appearance but only for his respectable character. However, now that he was king many began to fear that outsiders would judge their new king's exterior bitterly and not give him the respect deserved of a king.

The king's kind-hearted mother had educated her son well, cultivated his heart and mind and shaped him into an intelligent and compassionate man. The villagers had learned to look past the shock of his appearance to see only the good man he was. The man was liked by all but as their new king, fear mongers began speaking venomous words and calling their new king an ugly fool who would cause their kingdom's demise.

The New King was unaware of the cruel words being spread and ruled from his wise heart and mind making changes that immediately benefited all in the kingdom. With his leadership, wealth was distributed, all were paid handsomely for their work, and all were given a platform to speak their requests. He made sure that each family had plentiful food and necessities and once a month he invited everyone, including the peasants and guards, for a celebration at the castle. His leadership strengthened the kingdom and it soon was the strongest in the land. No one in the kingdom could refute that the new king had raised their dismal kingdom to previously unseen splendor. All were happy and strong.

Word spread to the neighboring kingdoms of this transformation. One king decided he must meet the king who had brought prosperity and joy to his people. The neighboring king arrived with a parade of horse-pulled carriages filled with gifts for the new king. The new king waited to greet the visitors at his throne. A long line of gift-carrying servants followed behind the visiting king as he walked toward the new king waiting. It was only when they were quite close that the new king's face became clear.

Not prepared for such a sight, the visitors gasped and covered their eyes. A box full with silver dropped to the floor and a shiny silver platter fell at the new king's feet. He bent to retrieve it and saw his reflection for the first time. He gasped before throwing the platter and running to his room, staying locked there for days into weeks. He refused to leave, proclaiming he was unable to lead with such terrible deformities and banned anyone from ever seeing him again. As he hid, the kingdom failed. Inner fighting began, robbers stole, hoarders hoarded and the strong ruled over the weak returning to the cruelty they had known before.

Finally, the king's mother broke into the room to see her son. Her son was venomous and pained as he scorned his mother for her lies and betrayal. "All of my life you made me believe I was special. You deceived me my whole life!"

"Deceived you? How?" The mother replied.

"You told me I was beautiful and convinced me that I was able to do anything I put mind and efforts into. You told me if I was kind, kindness would be returned to me even when I did not see it coming. You told me that I could make others better by showing my true self and believing in them as you believed in me. You made me believe that if I believed, things would happen but in truth I am an ogre! And all have been mocking me all along!"

The mother scorned her son and said, "Don't you ever call my son, our king, an ogre. I raised you to be blind to superficial judgment and clear to truth. Until you are that man again you deceive yourself!" The king's mother left with tears in her eyes and heart.

The more days passed the more the kingdom fell into chaos and the people yearned for their new king to return. It had become abundantly clear that all would be lost without his leadership to guide them. They begged to see him, sent letters and pleaded with the guards to no avail. Finally, they came together with a plan. If they could pile all of their belongings into a huge heap, someone could climb the pile and reach the king's window to deliver their plea.

They joined together sacrificing jewels, furniture, food and anything they had and threw it on the pile. When the pile was full of all of the material things in the kingdom it was still not quite high enough to reach the tower window, so they stacked upon each other until one little girl balanced high on top and yelled into the New King's window . . . "Please, please Sir King, Your Heinous we all need you!" The king came to the window. His heart beat full in his chest when he saw what all of the people of his kingdom had done to convince him of his importance and influence. He realized his shortsighted judgment of himself and promised to return to acting as their king immediately.

Indeed, his mother was right. True power is through strength of character — and who is it that shalt judge image anyway?

Thought:

All of us experience self-doubt in moments that we question our abilities. This is a normal part of assessing information about our environment and our position in it, however, self-doubt left unresolved quickly becomes self-defamation and must be eliminated! If you believe in yourself others will also. The influence of superficial judgments must not be internalized. Remember, image is illusion of the imagination while character is created from results of action. Image is empty. Character is indispensable.

Inquiry:

1. Are you self-conscious of anything (appearance, bad habits/thoughts, your past)?

2. Does that affect your confidence? Do you try to mask those aspects of yourself?

3. If you are criticized, do you take it personally? Do you amplify it with your own beliefs?

4. Can you hear someone in your childhood criticizing you? Is or was that person(s) important to you? Can you now hear their words as reflections of their own insecurities?

5. Do you find that you get caught in exterior evaluations and image rather than focus on substance of character? Why?

6. What are your strongest and most powerful abilities that you can use to inspire others?

Summary:

Know who you are. Ultimately nobody can answer for you who you are or who you want to be, other than you. What we all must do for ourselves is take the time to pause every now and again to review our beliefs and habits. To refresh the "why" in what we do. If that "why" aligns with our intentions, values, desires, and personal beliefs then we create behaviors that are consistent with an accurate depiction of who we choose to be.

II. Explore What You Believe

"Whether you think you can, or think you can't —

you are right."

— Henry Ford

What do you believe? Belief is a curious thing, though invisible it is as powerful as any other force affecting us. Our beliefs direct everything we do, how we feel and how we think. Our concepts of self and our environment are based in what we believe and yet our beliefs are built upon other people's ideas. Those kernels of opinion told to us from infancy onward grow into the principals we use to guide our daily living. Family traditions, religious commandments, and community laws are some of the dictators for how we express our self in the world and how we judge others and the situations we encounter. These belief systems were formed long before we were born and are not of our own invention. So what beliefs are our own?

Story 1

Elephant Ties

Adaptation of widely told story, author unknown.

A mother and son were at the circus. Before the show began, they took a walk to see the animals. The boy was very excited to see the elephants. When they came to the elephants the mother was astonished to see the large animals were standing, secured to only a weak chain connected to a stake in the ground. It was immediately clear to the woman that at any given moment these elephants could get free.

Concerned, the mother asked the trainer why there were no heavy chains or cages holding the animals back. She feared these powerful animals could escape their bonds and run free at any time and was confused as to why they didn't.

The trainer explained to the woman that that the elephants did not try to escape because they didn't believe that they could. The elephants had learned to believe they were incapable of obtaining freedom, unaware of their own strength and ability. Brought into the circus as smaller animals, the weak chains were adequate to hold them in place. The baby elephants tried to escape over and over again but with time they stopped trying. Not realizing their increasing power, the elephants believed they were incapable.

They stopped trying. Though they were powerful they decided they were weak. They no longer tried to be free because they didn't believe in their true power.

Thought:

Beliefs can empower and they can restrain. When we become aware of which beliefs hold us back, we can break free from those invisible ties. Positive beliefs can confine as well as negative ones by creating expectation. Expectation limits potential to become different than we predict and allow the many possibilities for expression in an experience. By removing limiting beliefs, we are free to explore our abilities and embrace our true power.

Inquiry:

1. What do you believe about yourself?

2. What labels do you use to describe yourself to others?

3. Do you know which beliefs limit you and which beliefs boost your personal power?

4. Can you remember how those beliefs were incorporated into your way of thinking?

5. What have you stopped trying at? Why? What do you believe you can't do or aren't good at?

6. Is there possibility you are wrong, and you can?

Story 2

The Cracked Pot

Adaptation of folktale, unknown author.

A peasant woman living in a rural village had two large pots, one hung on each end of a pole, which she carried across her shoulders. One of the pots had a crack in it while the other pot was perfectly intact. The perfect pot always delivered a full portion of water at the end of the long walk from the stream to its master's house, but the cracked pot arrived only half full. For many years this went on daily, with the woman delivering only one and one half pots of water to her home.

The perfect pot was proud of its accomplishment, perfect to the end for which it was made but the poor cracked pot was ashamed of its own imperfection and miserable that it was only able to accomplish just half of what it had been made to do. After numerous years of what it perceived to be failure, the broken pot spoke to the woman, "I am ashamed of myself and I want to apologize to you."

The woman was surprised but responded, "Why? What are you ashamed of?"

The pot explained, "For all of these years I have been only able to deliver half of my load because this crack in my side causes water to leak out all the way back to your home. Because of my flaws you have to do all of the work and you don't get the full value from your efforts."

The woman felt compassion for the old, cracked pot and pointed out to the pot, "Notice the beautiful flowers along only your side of the path."

Indeed, as they went up the hill the old, cracked pot took notice of the beautiful colored wildflowers on its side of the path. This cheered it some but at the end of the trail it still felt bad because it had leaked half its load again and so it again apologized to the woman for its failure.

The woman said to the pot, "You notice that there were flowers only on your side of the path but not on the other pot's side? That is because I have always known about your crack and

I took advantage of it. I planted flower seeds on your side of the path and every day while we walked back from the stream you have watered them. For all of these years I have been able to pick these beautiful flowers to decorate my family table. Without you being exactly as you are, we would not have this beauty to grace our home."

Thought:

Celebrate being just the way you are. If we did not have unique differences all would be the same with nothing spurring variety or interest. A single dimensional existence would offer little creativity or invention. We are incited, motivated, angered, impassioned and bettered by each other's contributions. Celebrate the color you bring to the path you travel!

Inquiry:

1. Do you tend to focus on what you believe you don't do well versus what you do well?
2. Do you believe you do a good job in the roles and responsibilities you take on?
3. Do you embrace your unique characteristics and believe they are contributive assets?
4. Can you identify at least three of your "differences" that you believe both positively and negatively impact those you interact with?
5. Are you more or less accepting of other's "cracks" than your own? Why?
6. What are three beliefs about yourself important to you?

Story 3

The Real Experience

"It makes no difference if the thing you believe is true..."
— Maya Angelou

Consider this statement. Notice your initial reaction. Reconsider. Here are three vignettes to present different views.

1. Shari's first holiday party at the new firm was joyful. Her coworkers all greeted her with friendly and welcoming smiles and handshakes, but one person made it special. She spent the most time with Bob, who was friendly and funny and entertained Shari all night with office stories and employee gossip. They laughed and talked for most of the evening. Shari was expecting they would exchange information, but she was pulled away by other coworkers before she could say good-bye. When she returned, Bob was gone. Shari enjoyed

Bob and was sure he enjoyed her. Her first holiday party was an occasion she would always remember fondly, and she considered Bob a friendly gentleman.

2. Ted had the best dad. His dad had always been a great coach, smart guide and wise in many varied areas including books and outdoors. His dad was always available to talk and was a fun companion when around. It was his dad that Ted called when he had questions about girlfriends and his teammates. His dad always had good advice. Ted was going to miss his best friend more than words could express.

3. She would always love her son. Patty could recall all of the ages bundled into one young man. His first steps, the sound of his baby giggle were still somehow part of him when she looked into the eyes of the 5'10" man who now looked back at her. She thought of the way he held her tight when he

was pried off of her to go to his first day of nursery school and the way he waved confidently as he left her to go to college. He was a loving son.

These are the truths of these individuals. All of the stories have what is common in all stories . . . they are interpretations. What you perceive and believe your experience to be, becomes your truth. But there are simultaneous truths. Let's use the above stories as examples. Here are alternative perspectives.

1. Bob was considered by most to be a jerk. He spoke poorly of his interaction with Shari, and women in general, but Shari never knew that, so she continued to enjoy her own perception of Bob and that evening. It stayed uncontaminated by anyone else's views and she held the joyful belief she had created.

2. Ted's dad had another family he had secretly managed for 30 years that Ted never knew about. His father stayed the pure image of the father that

Ted experienced him to be, uncomplicated by the additional facts, because Ted never learned of his father's alternate life, but it existed.

3. Tommy was a drug addict and criminal. His mother could see the sports injury that triggered the spiral into another existence with addiction but that didn't change what she knew in her heart. Her son was a prisoner now. He had done reprehensible things but she still could see his best qualities. She knew him as her loving son.

All of these stories did not change the truth of the experience . . . did they?

Perhaps it makes no difference if the thing you believe is true . . . to someone else.

Thought:

What you choose to believe becomes your truth. Truth is not absolute. There can be many co-existing truths for a single experience or condition. We think of truth and fact as being interchangeable, but they are not. Truth is malleable. It changes with individual. It changes with knowledge, perspective, time, environment, mood and ultimately choice.

Inquiry:

1. Do you believe truth is absolute or can truth change? Is it personal?

2. Can two people have conflicting definitions of truth for the same occurrence and both be true?

3. Can you think of something that you believed to be true when you were a child but as you matured that sense of truth changed? Were both points of view true to you at the time?

4. Are you able to influence truth?

5. Who determines the guidelines to label information true?

6. How does truth matter to you with others, and with yourself?

Story 4

The Two New Students

— LK

The math teacher announced to the class that there were two new students to their school in class and introduced them. After class, a girl went up to introduce herself to each new student separately. Both students asked the girl the same question, "What are the kids like at this school?"

The first new student didn't converse, he just asked her in an assertive tone, "What are the kids like at this school?"

The girl was surprised, they hadn't even finished with introductions. She considered before answering and decided to ask a question instead of answering directly. "Well, what do you think of the kids you have met so far?"

The new student responded right away, "Very rude and unfriendly. I think that the kids here seem stuck-up and think they are better than me."

The girl was taken aback, after all, she thought she was being friendly and had seen her classmates seem to be friendly also. She held her defenses and simply responded, "I am sorry to hear that. Unfortunately, you will likely find more of the same."

The next new student asked the very same question, but this student was smiling and seemed to be excited when asking, "What are the kids like at this school?"

After talking to the last student, the girl decided to ask the same question of this student, "Well, what do you think of the kids you've met so far?"

This student said, "So far everyone is really friendly and welcoming. I think the kids seem great!"

The girl happily responded, "I am happy to say that I am sure you will find more of the same!"

Thought:

As the old adage states, "seek and you shall find." Attitude is a great predictor of what you will experience in life. If you expect to find negativity, dishonesty and jealousy that is what you will get. If you travel forward with a loving heart, a compassionate mindset and an inviting attitude, you will find love, kindness, and opportunity welcoming you.

Inquiry:

1. Do you believe that your attitude impacts the reality you experience?

2. Do you believe more often you are cynical or accessible?

3. Do you think people respond differently depending on a person's attitude?

4. Are you skeptical of people who seem "nice"? Why or why not?

5. What would happen if you expected things to turn out better than you would predict?

6. How could you convey a better attitude in your life?

Summary:

Know what you believe. We might begin to wonder which beliefs are actually our own versus being trimmed down versions of what other people instilled in us. To begin to untangle that knot we must dedicate ourselves to reviewing and re-choosing the beliefs we feel align with our values and perceptions and discard those that do not. As Alice in Wonderland discovered, she was consistently changing, so are we. Like cleaning out closets, we must throw out beliefs that we have outgrown or worn too many holes in to serve our current needs and perspectives.

* Keep in mind, the identity we have fashioned is fragile. It is built upon a foundation of assumptions and opinions that we trusted as truth and use to make sense of our world. Beginning to dig into those frameworks can start a flurry of deeper questions. For some this is invigorating but for others it may feel like anxiety. If uncertainty begins to feel like stress ... pause ... breathe and pace your self-discovery in a way that makes you feel comfortable and still curious. Come back to generating more possibilities when you feel balanced and excited to do it. If these questions begin to cause deep discomfort in your life it is important to seek guidance and conversation with a specialist. This is your journey, enjoy it!

III. Take Responsibility for Your Choices

"If we hold on to our past we do it

at the expense of our future."

— TD Jakes

LAURA KITCH

Do you take responsibility for your decisions? Often people are tempted to attribute life position and outcomes to powers outside of their own control. It is easier to blame others, unfortunate timing, or bad luck instead of being accountable for your experiences. It's a way of giving up on yourself, not believing that you are capable of authority.

The stories in this segment remind us to take responsibility for our experiences. To learn from our mistakes, be aware of the situations we get into, notice how our actions impact others, and to step outside of comfort zones filled with excuses to go for what we want. Letting go of blame is not easy. Taking responsibility can be uncomfortable. If we don't do both, we sacrifice our own experience of life.

Story 1

Five Days Robbed

— LK

DAY ONE

Paul took the shortcut down the alley to get home.

He was pick-pocketed by a teenager hanging out there.

He didn't realize the alley got so dark and desolate.

It wasn't his fault.

DAY TWO

Paul took the same shortcut down the alley to get home.

He checked the alley first but didn't see the teen hiding in the darkness.

Again, Paul was pickpocketed.

He was furious with the teen.

DAY THREE

Paul took the same shortcut home down the alley to get home.

He brought a flashlight and put his wallet in his front pocket.

The teenager was hiding with a friend. One held Paul while the other took his wallet.

Paul realized he should have expected the teen would steal his wallet again.

DAY FOUR

Paul took the same shortcut home down the alley to get home.

He knew he shouldn't, but it was much faster.

He didn't bring his wallet. He brought a bat and a flashlight. He shouted to the teen and told him he had no money.

He walked through the alleyway, the teen stopped him and realized he really didn't have money.

The teen punched him for being foolish.

DAY FIVE

Paul took a different path home.

Thought:

If we choose to blame outside elements for our experiences and current position in life, we forfeit the power to change it. If instead, we embrace mistakes, failures or misguided attempts as reflections of our own choices, we can learn and adjust from those experiences and design better results in the future. Defeat or blame is replaced with confidence once we learn to trust our own abilities to adapt to the challenges we face. The stages of becoming self-aware are much like walking down the same alleyway expecting different results. Slowly we adjust until finally we don't repeat the negative pattern anymore.

Inquiry:

1. Do you take responsibility for where you are in life?

2. Do you tend to blame others? Why or why not?

3. Do you feel pride in the choices you make?

4. Can you identify which of your decisions led you to where you are now?

5. How could you better impact your current situation by being more responsible for your choices and the outcomes they create(d)?

Story 2

The Making of Rabbit Stew

— LK

There once was a fluffy bunny that hopped around getting into trouble wherever he went. One cold day he hopped through the forest and happened upon a large pot filled with water, set upon a big fire, arranged in the middle of a campsite deep in the woods. Nobody was around. The bunny searched everywhere but saw no one.

The bunny was cold so he stepped close to the fire. It felt wonderful. He considered the water would make for a warm bath. He jumped onto a nearby stump and reached as far as his little body could spread and dunked one toe into the water to check the temperature.

It wasn't hot at all. In fact, it was just lukewarm. The bunny decided a quick dunk wouldn't hurt anyone and would warm his body from the cold. He jumped in.

At first, the water felt amazing! It was a little tepid but better than outside in the cold.

After a short time the water warmed more and the bunny thought, this is divine.

Soon, the water became quite warm and soaked deep into his fur and soothed his bones. The bunny thought, this is quite warm, but relaxing indeed.

The bunny was extremely calm and didn't want to move. He felt the temperature of the water rising but he thought with a cloudy mind, just another moment and I will get out. As the water got hot the bunny was still reluctant to get out. A water bubble popped in the bunny's eye and he realized it was too hot and it was time to leave before he was boiled.

The bunny tried to move his legs but they were like molasses, his thinking was blurred and his body impossible to move. More bubbles popped all around him. The bunny tried to push a foot against the pot's bottom to push him out of the water, but the pot was too hot and burned his foot. He tried to grab the side edge of the pot to get out and singed his fur. It was impossible to get out now. The bunny had ignored all the signs that it was time to escape and had chosen to stay in the hot water too long. Now he was unable to move his body and was becoming drowsy and heavy and couldn't get himself out even as he began boiling. The campers returned to smell rabbit stew.

Had he waited too long? What was to become of him?

Thought:

Pay attention to the conditions you place yourself in and be responsible for how long you allow yourself to stay in damaging surroundings.

Inquiry:

1. Can you think of a situation in your life that you are currently in or were once in, that you stayed in after you knew you should leave? What happened?

2. If you are currently in an uncomfortable or unhealthy situation and can't get out on your own, have you asked for help? Who/where can you go to get help?

3. What will happen if you do not leave or change the conditions?

4. Why do you think people stay in bad or depleting situations? Do You?

5. How would you help another person to get out of a bad situation? How do you help yourself?

6. Is there an area in your life that conditions are hot, and the situation cannot be changed? *GET OUT!* *BEFORE* the water boils and you are stewed!

**If you need help call 911 or
the abuse hotline: 1-800.799.SAFE (7233)**

Story 3

Nails in the Fence

Adaptation of story heard. Similar version is in Steve Job's biography, written by Walter Isaacson.

There once was a little boy who had a bad temper. His Father gave him a bag of nails and told him that every time he lost his temper, he must hammer a nail into the back of the fence.

The first day, the boy nailed 37 nails into the fence.

Over the next few weeks, as he learned to control his anger, the number of nails hammered daily gradually dwindled down. He discovered it was easier to hold his temper than to drive those nails into the fence.

Finally, the day came when the boy didn't lose his temper at all. He was proud to tell his father he had succeeded. He told his father and the father suggested that the boy now pull out one nail for each day that he was able to hold his temper. The boy was disappointed but did as he was told.

The days passed and the young boy was finally able to tell his father that all the nails were gone. The father then took his son by the hand and led him to the fence. He said, "You have done well, my son, but look at the holes in the fence. The fence will never be the same. When you say things in anger, they leave a scar just like this one. You can put a knife in a man and draw it out. But it won't matter how many times you say I'm sorry, the wound will still be there. A verbal wound is as bad as a physical one."

The boy became a man who never forgot the lesson his wise father had bestowed him.

Thought:

Our actions and re-actions leave impressions on others that cannot be erased. The scars of our anger or unkindness remain long after the lashing is complete. We are all responsible for the imprint our reactions and actions leave on those around us. We are responsible for how we act, what we say, and how we use silence to be complicit in hurtful events.

Inquiry:

1. Can you identify a situation when your negative behavior impacted someone else? How about your inaction?
2. Did you consider that affect at the time, later on, or never?
3. Do you see how that scar will remain in some form even after the interaction has passed?
4. Can you identify how someone else's reaction(s) have left an imprint on you? Does that person know how they impacted you?
5. Do you hold yourself responsible for the impact you have on others? Can you be more aware?
6. Do you hold others accountable for the imprints they left on you? Can you forgive them?

Story 4

Searching for Keys in the Light

Adaptation of parable told through generations.

Nasrudin Hodja is said to have been a Sufi born in what is now modern day Turkey. He is used as a character of a philosopher and fool in numerous parables dating back to the 13th century. Nasrudin (one of many spellings) teaches us wisdom through jest of the obvious.

One day a student saw Nasrudin on his hands and knees under a streetlamp searching for something. "What are you searching for Sufi?"

"My keys."

The man joins Nasrudin on his hands and knees to search. After a good while the man asks Nasrudin, "Sufi, do you remember where about you lost them?"

Nasrudin responds, "Why yes, I dropped them near my house."

The man is confused. "Well then why are we searching here, nowhere near your house?"

Nasrudin continues his search as he answers, "Because this is where the light is."

Thought:

The easy solution often brings ineffective results, and avoidance little insight. Be it laziness or fear that makes us look in only in the safe and "well-lit" areas for answers, it will leave us at a loss for what we search to find. We must leave the security of the comfortable and the familiar if we seek change.

Inquiry:

1. Do you tend to stay "safe" in life? Why do you take that approach?

2. Do you avoid asking yourself tough questions?

3. What are you afraid of facing?

4. Do you tend to stay comfortable versus challenge yourself in life?

5. How do you deal with being uncomfortable (physically, emotionally, mentally)?

6. Are you willing to search in potentially darker spaces (less favorable, more disruptive parts of yourself and your history) and dive into the unknown to learn?

Summary:

Take Responsibility for your choices. Assigning blame or cause to external sources relinquishes the power to make change for yourself. We become servants to the undoing of our individuality and become chained to other people's vision. If we do not take responsibility for our choices and actions, then we forfeit that power to someone else instead of being the creators of our own life experience.

IV. Build Support for What You Want

"Remember no one can make you feel inferior

without your consent."

— *Eleanor Roosevelt*

"Go where you are celebrated

not where you are tolerated."

— *Unknown*

Do the environments and the people you surround yourself with make you stronger and inspire you? How do you spend most of your time, with who, and doing what? Do the people who you spend the most time with fuel you, inspire you to challenge yourself, and appreciate your uniqueness? Do the jobs you spend most of your time doing positively impact important aspects of your life? The people we spend the most time with and give our attention to, should be those people who we trust, admire, enjoy and respect most. They should bring us energy instead of draining us of our own. Where we spend our time should serve our personal goals and strengthen what is important to us. Designing the supportive environment that propels you toward getting what you want in life is a critical piece in creating personal happiness and achieving your vision.

Story 1

Two Lessons on the Energy in Life

Summary and adaptation from Jill Bolte Taylor's book,
"My Stroke of Insight: A Brain Scientist's Personal Journey."

In the book, *My Stroke of Insight: A Brain Scientist's Personal Journey*, neuroscientist Dr. Jill Bolte Taylor wrote of the insights she gained after suffering a debilitating stroke. During her stroke and through her recovery process, Dr. Bolte Taylor becomes acutely aware that everything is energy and that we are responsible for managing the energy that we distribute in life as well as the energy we allow to be taken or given to us by others.

This book is filled with informative insights based in science and personal experience but I am touching on just two of the many lessons that are specific to energy. The first transformative insight that the doctor shares with us in the book is when she realizes she needs to be responsible for preserving her own energy. This insight occurs as she is being wheeled into the emergency room and she notices her faculties are diminishing rapidly. From her training she knows that the shutting down of her brain is imminent and she must preserve any energy she has left by controlling her distribution of it. All mental effort must be carefully reserved, even her thinking process, for only the most urgent uses.

Well-intentioned nurses and doctors kept asking Dr. Bolte Taylor the same questions over and over again and she quickly realized that she must only provide the critical information and store the rest of her energy to heal. She realizes, it is up to her to protect her energy. She decides to not answer the nurses' requests anymore, determining that the demands of other people cannot be allowed to diminish her critical mental supply. This lesson is intensified in urgent conditions but incredibly important as a daily consideration for all. We are responsible for the care of and how we give away our critical energy.

Lesson 1: Preserve your energy to be used for purpose not filler. You are responsible for how you give your energy away to others. Be conscientious of how you distribute your force.

As Dr. Jill Bolte Taylor's mental capacity completely

diminishes she ends up in a coma. None around her believe she is able to perceive, never mind understand, her surroundings. The science states that with that part of her brain damaged she would not be aware. After recovering, Jill recounts that transcendental time and tells of a different type of awareness that she discovered. Though not able to speak, move, or indicate to outsiders that she had any mental abilities at all, she in fact *did*.

Her perceptions had moved away from language and labels and into energy fields. She identified visitors not by name or face but by the energy aura surrounding them. These "fields" of energy were individual and she recognized them rather than the names or faces of the actual people. For example, her mother was a very positive force that brought a sense of encouragement to Jill as well as those around her but Jill had no understanding that it was her mother who she sensed.

Names, titles, words all meant nothing to her in this state. Dr. Bolte Taylor then shares a very impactful experience that brought her professional, as well as personal, insight. She recounts two particular nurses that cared for her who were very different in their energy current. One nurse (who Dr.

Bolte Taylor identified as being similar to how she was as a practitioner prior to the stroke) was abruptly efficient and of a cold and distant energy. This nurse, like everyone else, believed that Jill was completely unconscious and unaware in every way. She treated Jill as an unemotional being and carried out the required treatment with understandable detachment. Jill felt a negative energy from this aura and felt her own energy decline when this nurse entered the room.

On the opposite spectrum was another nurse. This nurse also believed that Jill had absolutely no understanding of her surroundings or self but this nurse continued to treat Jill as a patient of full consciousness. This aura carried a positive energy into the room and Jill felt her own energy increase when this nurse entered. This nurse would ask Jill's permission before lifting her arm or explain to Jill what she was doing before she did it. This nurse (as did Jill's mother) talked to her and treated her with dignity and respect throughout the recovery (which nobody thought was to be a recovery) and Jill somehow felt it!

Though science had determined Dr. Bolte Taylor was unable to be aware of anything while in her coma, after her recovery she knew details about conversations, the people who had been near her, and things done to her. It is an important reminder, on so many levels, to always be responsible with your energy and compassionate with your actions at all times — even when you don't think others are aware.

In this recounting of the two different types of nurse's energy Jill teaches us important lesson #2.

Lesson 2:

"There are two types of people in this world, those who bring energy and those who take it away."
— *Dr. Jill Bolte Taylor*

Urgent circumstances forced Dr. Jill Bolte to take a clear look at the energy that people brought to her or took away from her, but the insight is a critical lesson to us all even when in very different situations. Assessing honestly the people that we surround ourselves with, the environments we place ourselves in, and the lack of regard we place on energy management can help us to improve and manage our physical and mental health much better.

Thought:

No Energy Suckers allowed! Be responsible for the energy you bring to a situation and also the energy you allow to be taken from you. It is easy to overlook the dynamic that you exist in. Family members, partners, friends, co-workers, etc. have consistent influence on the state of our personal energy. If we are in negative situations we will feel drained and unhealthy but if we foster healthy and mutually giving relationships that energy will help us to thrive. Be sure your tank is always being refueled not just emptied.

Inquiry:

1. Are you aware of your current energy level? Do you know when your levels rise and fall?

2. Are you clear on the type of energy you bring into a room or to the situations of your life?

3. Do the five people you spend the most time with make you feel stronger, joyful and energized? If not, why do you spend so much of your time with them?

4. Can you identify five people in your life that make you feel powerful? Five people who make you feel drained? How can you spend more time with the people who bring you power?

5. Do you feel responsible for the energy you bring to your situations?

6. How can you adjust to be more responsible for the energy you contribute?

Story 2

Know Your Friends

Two Men and the Bear, an Aesop Fable.

Two men were strolling down a forest path when they came across a bear. One man scampered up a tree and escaped the bear's claws, knowing his friend could not climb but climbing anyway. The other man knew there was nothing he could do, so he dropped to the ground and played dead.

The bear went up to the man and sniffed about his ears. He pawed at him a few times. Thinking the man was dead, the bear walked away.

After the bear left, his friend came down from the tree. "What did the bear say to you, friend, when he whispered in your ear?" asked his friend.

"Oh," answered his friend, "He just told me that I should consider about traveling with friends who run out on their friends in times of trouble."

Thought:

Know who your true friends are and be a true friend in return. We will have many acquaintances during our lifetime but fewer real friends. A true friend celebrates and supports you, protects your best interest, and shares his or herself with you sincerely. Being a true friend demands dedication of time and energy. That mutual commitment is special and must be given priority in life.

Inquiry:

1. Who are your true friends? Why do you trust them?

2. Do find that you mistake acquaintances as true friends?

3. Can you deepen the relationship with those people who you believe are invested and supportive of you? How?

4. Who are you a true friend to?

5. Would they count you as one of their true friends? Why or why not?

6. How do you show friends that you value your relationship?

Story 3

The Furniture Makers

— LK

Two sons and a father lived close to each other and worked together in the family furniture making business. One son was a light-hearted and calm woodcarver while the other was hotheaded and angry welder. Both were good men with different temperaments and were valuable creators of the furniture they made together.

Their father loved both sons dearly but as he got older and became weak with age he knew that he would need to figure out whom to leave his business to when he died. That day finally came. The father had left behind strict orders for the calm woodcarver to be fair and take care of the hotheaded welder brother when he signed the title of the business over to only the woodcarver son. He feared the welder's bad temper and related bad choices would ruin the business.

The woodcarver had fully planned to be fair but when the welder heard of their father leaving the business in only his woodcarving brother's name, he became furious. The hotheaded welder said terrible things to his brother and vowed to never speak to him again and stormed away.

The calm woodcarver hoped that his brother would simmer down and come back when his fury had passed but that didn't happen. The woodcarver tried many times to reach out to his brother but was only met with fury and rejection. Months passed and it was too long for the woodcarver to bear. He decided to make a peace offering and take it to his brother to mend their differences.

The woodcarver worked tirelessly, day and night for three days straight. When he was done he held in his hand the most beautiful, ornate wooden music box that when opened played a song their father used to sing when he worked. The woodcarver was hopeful that it would make his brother tender.

The woodcarver walked to the welder's shop to give his brother his gift. When he arrived his brother was busy welding.

The welder lifted his mask and with angry eyes growled an inquiry as to why his brother had come. The woodcarver presented his gift with an optimistic heart. The angry welder brother took the detailed wooden box and immediately placed it on the table before him and set his blowtorch to it. The delicate music box burned to a crisp before the woodcarver's words could stop it.

The woodcarver cried.

"Now you know how I feel!" yelled the welder.

"I am sorry brother. I was hoping that the gift and the title signed over to you inside would make you happy."

The welding brother inflamed with even more ferocious anger. He yelled at his brother for being so stupid to not tell him that the title was inside. He cursed his brother and sent him away with orders to never come back.

The woodcarver was broken-hearted and when he returned to the village he immediately went to seek the guidance of the wisest woman in the town. He explained all that had happened, their father dying, the business being left in only his name, the gift with the title inside burned by his angry brother. He explained his heartache and expressed that he thought it might be just too much for him to handle.

The woman advised him that that his brother's anger was not his to bear. "Even if a gift is given with the very best intentions it still may be that the receiver is not ready to receive it. A gift not received is not a gift at all."

She then explained, "It is also the same in reverse. Just because someone hands something to you doesn't mean that you need to accept it. When you brother gives you his anger you do not need to accept it. Think of it as a box filled with rotten garbage that you have no use for…you leave it behind and it remains his to keep, not yours to take."

The brother felt relieved. He left the anger, pain and resentment that was not his behind and moved forward in his life. Months later his brother came to re-unite. The brother explained that a wise woman had happened into his welding shop in need of a fix and through their conversation she had made him realize all he had lost due to his anger. The wise woman had convinced him to try to mend differences.

The woodcarver welcomed his brother with open arms, and they reunited as family and also as business partners. The brothers built beautiful furniture together, honored to carry on the name of their noble father. Their business thrived, their families joined, and their love grew.

Thought:

A gift is both given and received. Either contributor can choose to not participate. This premise applies to items and reactions. Be it love or misgivings it is up to both participants to determine which pieces they will give and/or accept. Be sure of your responsibility in each role.

Inquiry:

1. What have you accepted from another that you did not want (a gift, bad energy, burden of their bad choice)?

2. Did you minimize your power by choosing to accept it?

3. When people put their weight on your shoulders do you feel able to reject that burden?

4. Have you put your burdens onto someone else without considering their feelings?

5. When you give your time or attention to someone do you consider if they are receiving it the way you intended to provide it?

6. What can you do in your own life to better notice the balance of giving and receiving?

Story 4

Reconsidering the Three Little Pigs

Adaptation of story by James Halliwell-Phillipps
as most recognizably told by Joseph Jacobs in,
English Fairytales.

Most of us have heard this fairytale before. How can you hear it differently?

Once upon a time there was an old mother pig who had three little pigs and not enough food to feed them. So when they were old enough, she sent them out into the world to seek their fortunes.

The first little pig was very lazy. He didn't want to work at all and he built his house out of straw. The second little pig worked a little bit harder but he was somewhat lazy and he built his house out of sticks. Then, they sang and danced and played together the rest of the day.

The third little pig worked hard all day and built his house with bricks. It was a sturdy house complete with a fine fireplace and chimney. It looked like it could withstand the strongest winds.

The next day, a wolf happened to pass by the lane where the three little pigs lived; and he saw the straw house, and he smelled the pig inside. He thought the pig would make a mighty fine meal and his mouth began to water.

So he knocked on the door and said:

"Little Pig! Little Pig! Let me in! Let me in!"

But the little pig saw the wolf's big paws through the keyhole, so he answered back:

"No! No! No! Not by the hairs on my chinny, chin, chin!"

Then the wolf showed his teeth and said:

"Well then I'll huff and I'll puff and I'll blow your house down!"

So he huffed and he puffed and he blew the house down! The wolf opened his jaws very wide and bit down as hard as he could, but the first little pig escaped and ran away to hide with the second little pig.

The wolf continued down the lane and he passed by the second house made of sticks; and he saw the house, and he smelled the pigs inside, and his mouth began to water as he thought about the fine dinner they would make.

So he knocked and he said:

"Little Pigs! Little Pigs! Let me in! Let me in!"

But the little pigs saw the wolf's pointy ears through the keyhole so they answered back:

"No! No! No! Not by the hairs on our chinny, chin, chin!"

So the wolf showed his teeth and said:

"Then I'll huff and I'll puff and I'll blow your house down!"

So he huffed and he puffed and he blew the house down! The wolf was greedy and he tried to catch both pigs at once, but he was too greedy and got neither! His big jaws clamped down on nothing but air and the two pigs scrambled away as fast as their little hooves would carry them.

The wolf chased them down the lane and he almost caught them. But they made it to the brick house and slammed the door closed before the wolf could catch them. The three little pigs they were very frightened, they knew the wolf wanted to eat them. And that was very, very true. The wolf hadn't eaten all day and he had worked up a large appetite chasing the pigs around and now he could smell all three of them inside and he knew that the three little pigs would make a lovely feast.

So the wolf knocked on the door and said:

"Little Pigs! Little Pigs! Let me in! Let me in!"

But the little pigs saw the wolf's narrow eyes through the keyhole, so they answered back:

"No! No! No! Not by the hairs on our chinny, chin, chin!"

So the wolf showed his teeth and said:

"Then I'll huff and I'll puff and I'll blow your house down!"

Well! He huffed and he puffed. He puffed and he huffed. And he huffed, and huffed, huffed and he puffed, puffed; but he could not blow the house down. At last, he was so out of breath that he couldn't huff and he couldn't puff anymore. So he stopped to rest and thought a bit.

But this was too much. The wolf danced about with rage and swore he would come down the chimney and eat up the little pigs for his supper. But while he was climbing on to the roof the little pig made a blazing fire and put on a big pot full of water to boil. Then, just as the wolf was coming down the chimney, the little piggy pulled off the lid, and plop! The wolf fell into the scalding water.

So the little piggy put the cover on again, boiled the wolf up, and the three little pigs ate him for supper.

Thought:

It is important to be wise and hardworking while building a supportive environment, but it is just as important to remember to be compassionate when you are the one in the brick house. Practicality leads us toward success, hard work helps us achieve it, and kindness enables us to appreciate and forgive, so we aren't alone there.

Inquiry:

1. Do you feel that you are a hard and smart worker? Do you value those characteristics?

2. Do you judge other people for playing instead of working?

3. Do you balance work and play well?

4. Do you feel you build sturdy supportive structures in your life (physical and social)?

5. The Big Bad Wolf represents the fears we allow to threaten our sense of safety. What would a fear be you have in life? Is your fear just a big bad wolf that doesn't really exist outside of your imagination?

6. Another important lesson in this fairytale is to be generous with others less fortunate than you. Do you consider yourself generous? Do you surround yourself with people who are generous toward you?

Summary:

Build support for what you want. Choose people and environments that fuel you and provide you with the power to become stronger and more resolutely your unique self. Making changes to the way you focus your time and energy takes hard work. Moving toward something requires moving away from something else. On your way to better remember to look back fondly and appreciate the past that drove you forward while opening your arms to welcome the present you created.

As Farrah Gray stated:

"Build your own dreams or someone else will hire you to build theirs!"

V. Trust Yourself

"Believe you can and you're halfway there."

—*Theodore Roosevelt*

Do you believe you *can*? Self-doubt is our strongest adversary. It distorts all areas of life if we allow it to have power. Self-doubt is different than being uncertain in a situation or feeling hesitant to perform a risky action. Self-doubt is when we embrace and reinforce insecurities regarding our abilities and value. If you have a consistent, underlying feeling that you are not good enough, or that you aren't worthy of positive attention, kind nurturing or even nice things in your life it is important to seek professional guidance. When we don't feel deserving of good and we don't trust our inner wisdom, we are inadequately serving the precious life we have been given to live. Believe in yourself first so that you can believe in others next.

LAURA KITCH

Story 1

A Subway Ride

— LK

My cousin came in to visit New York City from Iowa. She was about twelve then. She came with her mother and a friend. My father lived in the city and toured my cousin and her friend all around Manhattan and one day brought them out to Long Island to see the beach. My cousin hadn't ever been to the beach and also had never been on the subway.

My aunt told me the story of what happened to my cousin and her friend on their way to the beach and included her own wisdom. My cousin, Kathy, and her friend, Maddie, went along with my father to catch a subway to Penn Station where they were taking a train to Long Island. As they waited on the busy platform the subway train pulled up and a herd of people got off the train and walked between Kathy, Maddie and my father. The girls were confused and got on to the train thinking that my father had gotten on, but he had not.

The doors closed and the train rushed away. The platform cleared and there was no sight of my cousin or her friend. A wave of panic struck my father when he realized what must have happened. On the train my cousin and her friend searched for my father and realized that he was not there. They had stepped on to an express train and it was quickly passing by the next station stop so they screamed, "Help!" A person pulled the alarm and the train stopped!

To make the longer story shorter, Kathy and her friend were permitted to walk the side path through the tunnel back to the previous station (yes, really). They did reconnect with my father and continued on their day journey to visit the beach.

When they returned they told the story. My cousin Kathy thought that it was the most exciting adventure she had ever had. Joy spread across her face as she described the exploration through the tunnel and the nice man who escorted them to safety.

Maddie crunched her face and said, "It was horrible. We were soooo scared!" Kathy agreed as Maddie described her fear.

Maddie added, "It was disgusting in the tunnel and even all of the subway stations. They are filthy and tons of people are packed against each other like bundles of sticks." Kathy agreed as Maddie described the grunge and pushy people.

The recounting of the beach visit was similar. Kathy began by describing the ocean with awe and elation, while Maddie described it as huge and threatening. Kathy loved the soft sand and how it felt through her toes, while Maddie talked about how annoying the sand was sticking on her skin. Each time, Kathy adjusted her descriptions to concur with the alternative viewpoint of Maddie. Finally, my aunt couldn't stay quiet any longer and she blurted out,

"Kathy, I would like to hear you tell me, all on your own, your experience through your own words and then Maddie will tell her experience through her own words so I can listen to each of you fully."

Kathy had already been influenced and began with negative descriptions. My aunt stopped her and asked about the first words Kathy had used, "I recall you said the subway was exciting?"

Kathy responded on that thought, "Oh mom it was so fast. It felt like a rocket ship taking us somewhere magical!" But then she thought of what Maddie had said and Kathy added, "But it was scary when we thought we were lost."

My aunt acknowledged that must have felt unnerving but thankfully they were safe. Then she asked, "I remember you thought going through the tunnel felt like an adventure?"

Kathy returned to her sense of excitement and with the reminders my aunt offered, soon Kathy described a day filled with adventure, discovery, amazement and joy. Maddie chose her own version for her memory. My aunt reminded both girls to see life through their own eyes not someone else's.

Tell and live your story, not someone else's . . . and remember to forgive and be kind. Your memories will stay with you and build the story of your lifetime.

Thought:

Stay true to your own nature and independent perception when designing the memories of a lifetime.

Inquiry:

1. We are all influenced by those in our lives, be it family and friends, media, or co-workers. Can you spot the ways that your personal story and memories have been affected by and continue to be affected by others?

2. Can you identify areas and ways that you impact others in the forming of their memories?

3. What groups or communities are you affiliated with? How do those shared viewpoints influence your own interpretations (religious, ethnic, education, job, neighborhood, sports, music, etc.)?

4. Do you believe that how you see life, yourself, and others is a reflection of your memories?

5. How could you be more responsible for how you affect other people's memories?

6. How can you be more vigilant with how you build your own?

Story 2

The Trust Fall

Some ideas contributed from the reading of the book
Tuesdays With Morrie, *by Mitch Albom.*

There is an activity common in both sales trainings and team building seminars called the trust fall. It involves two individuals or more building trust by falling backwards into the support of the other individual or group. I have participated in this exercise and can attest to the impact it can make.

I recall an excerpt from the book *Tuesdays With Morrie*, by Mitch Albom that had a good take on this experience. In this book a terminally ill professor, Morrie, shares life insights with a visiting student, Mitch. One of the lessons Morrie imparts on his student is the importance of being in touch with what you feel.

Morrie tells of the exercise as he constructed it in one of his classes. He had students pair off and then taking turns one person would turn their back to the other student, walk away a bit and then fall back into the arms of the other student. It is an unnerving task, and most students struggled in performing this exercise. It sounds easy but to fall back blindly goes against our instincts.

Most students who did it hesitated, but one girl had no trouble at all. She met her partner, turned her back to the partner, walked steps away, closed her eyes, and instantly fell backwards into her partner's arms. The class was quite surprised by her trust. Morrie explained to the student, "You see, you closed your eyes. That was the difference. Sometimes you cannot believe what you see you have to believe what you feel. And if you are ever going to have other people trust you, you must feel that you can trust them too — even when you're in the dark. Even when you are falling."

In my experience, this exercise is titled well . . . *Trust Fall.* The question is, who is it that you are trusting? The answer may not be as obvious as it seems. Yes, you want to know that the "net" is structurally able to support your weight but once that information has been verified, the trust turns inward. Can you trust yourself to let go and know you are going to be ok? To realize that life is not as controllable as we like to believe can be unnerving but to know you will be ok anyway is to trust in your own abilities to adjust with the ebb and flow of life. We must trust ourselves to trust others.

Thought:

Trust comes from within first and then it can be extended toward others. It is important for all of us to find and value those people we trust in our lives. Those people who provide a safe and supportive place to "fall into" and know we will be cared for. It is equally important to be that place to others. Once we realize that we are capable of providing that place of trust to another we are able to believe that another can provide it to us in return. The old mantra that you must care and love yourself before you can care for and love someone else is another expression of the trust fall.

Inquiry:

1. Trust begins with belief in self. Do you trust yourself?

2. Are there areas you can identify that you don't trust yourself?

3. Who can you be completely vulnerable with?

4. Can you find more ways to build trust in your life?

5. Are you able to let go and trust?

6. Do you think it is ok to fall?

Story 3

A Chainsaw Moment

— LK

My friend who is a beautiful, petite person with a soft Oklahoma accent, surprises me regularly with her bold abilities. Just thinking about her makes me smile and reminds me how we all have a fiery power coursing through our spirit. Sometimes we just need to unleash it.

We met for dinner and my friend arrived with a wounded leg. I asked, "How in the world did you hurt your leg?" She rolled her eyes and laughed. Then she told a tale of ordinary proportion.

In New York we had some significant storms that left major damage to trees and houses in the area that year. Torrential rains had over-saturated the soil, exposing the root systems and weakening the already wind battered trees. The final punch came when a large windstorm blew through our area knocking down many of the trees that had been struggling to survive.

It was a mess! Countless people were left without electricity, had damage to their homes and property, and roads were blocked impeding the flow of traffic around town. Clean-up resources were overloaded with such high demand that everyone was forced to wait to clear their yards of debris.

My friend is very neat and orderly. The disorder in her yard was driving her mad but ultimately it was the incessant complaints of an ornery neighbor that got under her skin the most. A large branch had fallen off my friend's tree and across a fence that separated her yard from her neighbor's. This neighbor was insistent that my friend remove the branch immediately, which of course was not realistic. All services were booked and my friend's husband had been too busy to remove the tree branch, which meant she would have to do it alone. The branch was huge.

The irritating neighbor continued bothering my friend, sometimes multiple times in a day. The constant grievances eventually prompted my friend to react. "It happened in a burst," she explained. She was in her pajamas and slippers drinking her morning coffee when the rush of determination struck. My friend decided to take matters into her own hands in a moment we now refer to as a "Chainsaw Moment."

The thought of her neighbor's disapproving scowl had triggered my friend into action. Wearing her slippers and carrying her morning coffee, my friend went in to her garage and found her "husband's" chainsaw. She grabbed it in her free hand (coffee still in other), marched her way out into the yard and proceeded directly toward the rogue branch. She placed her coffee down and started the buzzing saw. Flecks of wood flew through the air as the saw jawed its way through the disassembled branch that rested across the fence.

My friend had adrenaline coursing through her body. She described feeling empowered as she completed the task all on her own. She was still proud of herself as she told me the story over dinner and I was proud for her too. We celebrated her Chainsaw Moment. She had taken matters into her own hands and resolved the situation without waiting for someone else to do it for her. And she had used a power tool to do it!

Neither of us had used a chainsaw before and it seemed an intimidating tool, which made it an even bigger accomplishment. She convinced me, "Using the saw was easier than expected. Even cutting through the thick wood was not hard." A revelation to us both. Suddenly the untouchable task we viewed as a job for someone else with more strength became accessible to us both. Her accomplishment had influenced my belief of my own capability as well. I believed I could do it too!

"But how did you hurt your leg?" I asked again, glad to learn she hadn't cut it with the saw.

"Oh yah that," she smiled. "After cutting the branch into a few pieces, removing whatever was in my neighbor's yard, I grabbed my coffee and started to head back to my house. I have to admit I was quite proud of myself. All was fine until my slipper got caught under a different fallen branch and I fell - twisting my ankle. It was so bad I had to go to the doctor after a few hours of swelling and pain." She winced, "sprained."

Thought:

Remember…you can do it! Don't wait for someone to do IT for you, do it yourself.

Inquiry:

1. Can you identify areas in your life that you step back and wait for someone else to do something that you could do yourself? If so, why?

2. Do you find that you question your capability to accomplish certain types of tasks?

3. Are you generally confident in your abilities?

4. Are you usually a doer or an observer? Do you believe that you could become more of a doer if you chose to?

5. Right now, are you avoiding doing something or waiting on someone else to finish or do *IT* for you?

6. Could you do it yourself? Why aren't you? Why *really* aren't you? Lazy? Insecure? Overwhelmed? Disorganized?

7. Can you make a Chainsaw Moment for yourself right now? A choice that empowers you.

Story 4

The Authentic You is Calling

Adaptation of many versions. Original author unknown. This is an alternate version of the story, The Eagle Who Thought She Was a Chicken.

The first version of *The Eagle Who Thought She Was a Chicken* ended with the eagle doubting her inner calling and neglecting her yearning to fly and be with the other eagles soaring through the sky. That Eagle died a chicken. Here is a different version.

As in the first version, the mother chicken raises the eagle as she did her other chicken babies. The eagle grew up thinking that she was a chicken. The eagle ignored her inner knowing that she was designed for a different life and listened to the others who told her that her dreams and desires were not attainable. Until . . .

One day, a park ranger came to the farm to see the eagle

he had heard behaved like a chicken. When he saw the strong and able creature stumbling around clumsily on the ground pecking for kernels of scattered corn, the ranger was upset and spoke to the farmer. "This great bird is intended to fly in the sky with the other eagles, not peck the ground with the chickens."

The farmer replied, "It is no longer an eagle, the bird is now a chicken. It has been raised a chicken and all it knows to be is a chicken."

The ranger lifted the eagle and put it on the fence, hoping it would spread its massive wings and fly. The eagle looked up to the sky and then to the ground. She hesitated before dropping down into the pen where it was comfortable to peck at the earth.

The ranger knew what this great bird was destined for and was saddened by its lack of confidence. He was determined to awaken her to her abilities and guide her toward her destiny. He carried the massive bird up to the rooftop of the barn and nudged her forward. As she came to the very edge of the roof, she gazed up to the beautiful blue sky where the other eagles flew above her and instinctively moved her massive wings.

There was a great stir and she hovered for a moment before she tucked her wings away and plopped back down into the pen to return to pecking.

The man was defeated and thanked the farmer for allowing him to visit. The farmer said, "I told ya', just another chicken!"

The man asked the farmer for one more visit, the farmer agreed and the next day the ranger came back to the farm with a great glove that covered his arm and took the eagle out of her pen and carried her all the way up the mountain top where he had noticed the other eagles returning to the day before. There he found the eagles' nest above a cliff. He climbed to that cliff, walked out as far out as he could, and stretched his arm over the side of the mountain. The clouds and energy of the other birds flying nearby brushed by the eagle on his arm. The ranger spoke to the eagle kindly, explaining that he knew the grand abilities she possessed and how she was destined to soar through the sky and reach the tops of mountains rather than walk inside a small pen filled with chickens and dried dirt. He promised her that he had faith in her abilities even when she did not and he was doing this for her sake. With that, he threw the eagle chicken off of the mountain.

At first she spiraled and fell like a boulder. The man's heart dropped heavy with regret and remorse . . . but then he saw it. A volcano of energy swelled inside of her. The eagle spread her massive wings and beneath the feathers emerged a powerful spirit that lifted that bird high in the sky. She flapped her grand wings and rose up toward the sun and glided along the mountaintops. The ranger filled with joy. He watched the eagle soar mightily through the sky authentic in her truth and abilities. She joined the other eagles and lived the rest of her life as an Eagle!

Thought:

Follow that which you know to be true in your heart even if those surrounding you disagree. No one can tell you who you are, though special ones may help to remind you. Sometimes it takes someone else to believe in us before we are able to believe in ourselves. Value those who are your champions and always strive to *soar!*

Inquiry:

1. Do you surround yourself with people who remind you of your power and abilities or deflate your ambitions?

2. Do you let fear keep you from pursuing your dreams?

3. Who pushes you forward to challenge yourself? Who wants to see you soar?

4. Do you try to avoid failure or judgment? At what cost?

5. What would it look like and feel like to you if you no longer let fear be an obstacle? What would that change in your life?

6. Where in your life do you choose to soar?

Summary:

Trust yourself! We all will experience times of failure, doubt or mistakes but if we allow that spore of doubt to fester it will spread and corrode our sturdy self. It is critical to promptly return to trusting yourself after stumbling off course. Navigating life from a core perspective of belief that you are able to adjust and overcome obstacles. Direct your attention to your strengths and positive qualities to stop the progression of self-defeating thoughts. Mindful care of mental chatter is essential to living a balanced and powerful life. Believe and trust in *you!*

VI. Commit to Positive Awareness

"If you don't like something, change it.
If you can't change it change your attitude."
— *Maya Angelou*

BLACK DOG ZEN

What is your general attitude toward life? Viktor Frankl was a well-known psychotherapist and philosopher. He was also a prisoner in a concentration camp who witnessed his entire family, with exception of his sister, and countless others get murdered in the Nazi camps. He sustained unimaginable physical and mental torture and suffered absolute despair, but he survived his circumstances through his search for meaning and his connection to love. He attributed human's ability for endurance to the ultimate freedom bestowed us, the freedom to choose one's attitude.

"Everything can be taken from a man but one thing: the last of the human freedoms — to choose one's attitude in any given set of circumstances, to choose one's own way."
—Viktor Frankl

Story 1

Monk With a Mirror

Adaptation of a Zen story of unknown origin.

A Monk and his disciple went for a long walk through the forest together. The student was excited to be in the company of the idyllic and distinguished monk and was hopeful to learn many things during their walk. The walk began with silence. The student had so many questions for his mentor but he thought it best to follow the actions of his guide and wait for an appropriate time to speak.

The walk continued in complete silence but the student noticed a disturbing habit of the master monk. The senior monk would walk without ever saying a word but twice he had reached into his robe and pulled out a mirror, which he checked his image in before putting it back into his robe and continuing forward in silence.

The student was horrified by his teacher's indulgence. It was an offense to succumb to vanity and look in mirrors. It showed concern for your own appearance. He felt soured inside and offended by his teacher's disregard for proper behavior. How could such a noble monk commit such a vain and unorthodox act? They continued in quiet until the student couldn't stand the anger festering inside of him. He burst out with his accusation in complete disregard for propriety and said to his guide, "Forgive me but I must ask sir, do you not feel shame in the vain indulgence of checking your looks in this mirror you carry when you know it is against our primary teachings not to embrace ego?"

The monk pulled the mirror from his bag and pointed it at the young student. Then he said, "I use it in times of trouble. I look into it and it shows me the source of my problems as well as the solution to my problems."

Thought:

We can only change our self. We must always return to holding our self accountable for our life and the experiences we are forming. It is our own thoughts and behaviors that are the determinants for how we interpret our experiences. Like the monk did when he became frustrated, instead of blaming others he returned to his own reflection as the source for his anguish as well as for his power to change.

Inquiry:

1. Do you look to yourself for answers to your discontent as well as your joy?
2. Are you able to critique your own actions?
3. Do you use silence to find clarity?
4. Do you believe that you are responsible for changing how you feel and behave?
5. How would your story change if you believed life was a story and you were authoring it?
6. What characters, experiences, feelings and challenges would you write into your life and which would
    you edit out?

Story 2

Two Lions

— LK

There were two male lion cubs that played together every single day. Both were equally able yet one was quiet and the other roared all of the time. As they bounced through the fields, jumped over rocks and rolled in playful fight one of the cubs remained quiet and the other sounded an endless roar. The loud lion loved to hear his own roar and roared all of the time while the other cub was far too busy exploring and was not interested in roaring for no cause. As time passed the quiet lion noticed that his roaring friend was often roaring with complaint. His friend complained if he was slower to capture prey or if he couldn't perform as well as the quiet lion in any way. The roaring lion became so focused on complaining he forgot about doing.

The quiet lion enjoyed doing and soon found the best way to do things was to do them without his complaining friend holding him back. He started going out for early treks alone before his complaining friend would wake. At first, the roaring lion would wake later than the quiet lion but still wanted to go out for play when he awoke but as time passed the roaring lion became lazy. He no longer wanted to leave his comfortable home to be disrupted by any uncomfortable conditions that an exploration might bring him and so he stayed with the pride all day, resting.

He still complained a lot about nothing of importance and from so much practicing of his roar, the roaring lion developed a full and ferocious sounding tone. Many in the pride started to treat him special. They assumed that his strong and powerful roar meant that he was a strong and powerful lion and many adorers would gather around the roaring lion to brush his fur or clean his claws as he rested contently.

The roaring lion enjoyed being pampered by others much more than doing and soon he decided to stay and be cared for rather than join his friend at all. As they matured they became more and more different. The roaring lion had formed an intimidating and full roar as he lay around having his needs met by others, while the quiet lion built an independent confidence by challenging his mind and body everyday. The quiet lion became a powerful and strong lion.

One day the quiet lion returned from his morning journey to find he was blocked from coming home. He was told that the roaring lion had become their new king since their old pride leader was too feeble to protect them anymore. The pride believed that the roaring lion's savage roar was proof of his bravery and competence and they chose him as their new king. There was only room for one head male so the roaring lion had roared that his friend should not be allowed back into the pride when he returned from his daily walk.

The quiet lion was surprised and hurt but did not complain, instead he walked away into the wild around him he had come to know so well. It was not long before he found another pride in need of a leader. The quiet lion had a strong body and great awareness of the habitat they lived in and made a great leader. He was very loved and respected by his new pride.

One day the quiet leader heard tale of a wounded, roaring lion in the field nearby. The quiet lion went to find the wounded lion and learned it was his old friend. Weak and mangy, the roaring lion barely roared a muffled account of his woes to his long-forgotten friend. "I was a fool, please forgive me before I die. I never should have sent you away. I always knew how much stronger and wiser you were than me and my arrogance got in my own way. Of course I was not mighty enough to protect my pride and a new stronger lion came and took over not long after you left. I have traveled all this way with only one intention, to apologize to my quiet and honorable friend." The once roaring lion then passed out.

The quiet leader lifted his friend by the nape of his neck and dragged him back to his new home. They fed and cared for him until he was healed and strong. When he awoke, the once roaring lion realized he had been saved by the very friend he had betrayed years before. He thanked his friend and prepared to leave.

"You are invited to stay and live in our pride," said the quiet leader.

"But there can not be two males in a pride dear friend," said the once roaring lion.

"No friend," corrected the king, "there can not be two leaders."

The once roaring lion smiled and bowed to his friend by lowering his head on his front paws. "I would be honored to live under you my king!"

They lived peacefully friends and neither roared in complaint.

Thought:

True bravery is often quiet in its delivery. Those who brag deplete the potency of their talent and the power of their influence by spending too much effort on self-promotion rather than skill. It is easy to be influenced by those who boast or complain with loud declaration but important not to succumb to that force of persuasion. Instead do and surround yourself with others who "do"! Those who only know how to roar will become transparent over time. True leaders will do.

Inquiry:

1. Are you a boaster? Do you like to speak of your successes or strengths?

2. Can you identify those who roar more than they do in your life? Are you one?

3. Are you powerful? Would others say you were powerful? Are you humble?

4. Do you enjoy the praise of others or feel uncomfortable with the attention?

5. Are there areas where you might benefit not roaring as much and begin doing more?

6. Do you respect your good friends?

Story 3

The Three Sand Players

Amalgamation of many stories and observation.

There were three children playing together in the sand. They were working together to bring wet sand up to a dry patch of ground away from the water's reach. Each took their pail and filled it with wet sand near the shoreline and walked it back up to the dry sand, flipped the bucket upside down, and patted the bottom for the wet sand to form a pile near a previous pile laid before.

A mother nearby watched the three children work together, each with a different attitude in what they were doing. She approached the three and asked each separately what they were doing?

The first child seemed to be enjoying the process the least. He grouchily stamped his feet and complained every time he returned to the water's edge to refill his bucket. The lady asked the boy, "What are you doing?"

Grouchily the boy grumbled, "Filling buckets with wet sand and dumping them on the dry sand. Its hard and it doesn't seem like it makes any difference anyway. The water keeps knocking them down."

The woman asked the next child who seemed content in the process, "What are you doing?"

He answered, "I am working on building a tall wall. It is tiring, but I love to see the wall get higher."

Then the lady asked the boy who was cheerfully running back to the water's edge from the dry sand over and over again each time smiling and running with abundant energy. The lady asked, "What are you doing?"

The boy smiled and with great excitement said, "Well I am helping to build the most wonderful skyscraper that has ever been made in the most magnificent city ever seen. The skyscraper has many rooms and a river around it. Can't you see?"

The woman smiled, "Indeed I can!"

Thought:

What are you building? Life is as much about the perceptions we adopt about what we are doing as it is the actions we perform. If we believe that our time is spent in tasks of subservience, then we stay prisoners to that fate. We will conclude that our efforts are tedious and insignificant and become embroiled in a monotonous and exhausting existence. However, if we interpret our efforts as being part of a larger significance, we find purpose in our contribution.

Inquiry:

1. How do you feel about the work you do in your life?

2. Do you work with a sense of vision or simply to complete tasks?

3. What are you building with the work you do?

4. Could you create purpose in your actions by making you vision bigger? What would that vision look like?

5. How can you change what you are building to have it feel more significant to you?

6. Are you moving wet sand or building skyscrapers?

Story 4

The Cave and the Sun

Author unknown, Sufi Story.

One day the sun and a cave had a conversation. The sun had trouble understanding what "dark" and "dreary" meant and the cave couldn't conceive what "light and bright" meant. They decided to visit each home to experience both.

Upon seeing where the sun lived the cave said to the sun, "This is wonderful. It is so joyful and clear here. I am ashamed to show you where I have been living." The sun was jubilant about visiting the cave's dwellings and entered with cheer. The cave felt a bit embarrassed at how cold and dreary his home was compared to the bright home of the sun. The sun quietly looked around, not wanting to say anything too quickly. The cave finally said, "I am sorry to bring you to such a depressing place. I should have been more considerate knowing the beauty you are used to living with."

LAURA KITCH

Then the sun replied, "I didn't want to appear rude but dear cave, I must admit, I don't see any difference."

Thought:

BYOS! Bring your own sunshine and light the places you go. If you come with a sunny disposition you will light the path forward and brighten the surroundings you encounter along the way.

Inquiry:

1. How do you choose to see life?

2. How do you shine light when experiencing moments of darkness?

3. Do you tend to succumb to the difficulties you experience or rise to shift the occasion?

4. What lifts you up when you are feeling low?

5. Could you find more "sunshine" to illuminate the obstacles you encounter?

6. How can you BYOS to your environment?

Summary:

Commit to positive awareness! If a person who is imprisoned in unbearable conditions can survive and find compassion and inspiration while suffering unthinkable torment, that means the choice is available to all. Most of us live in experiences that are not nearly as extreme as Viktor Frankl and yet we blame our circumstances for our state of being. If we retain our sense of responsibility for how we interpret the situations we encounter, we then become empowered to adjust our attitude and shed light on even the more dire conditions. A good attitude begins with refocusing on gratitude, love, and intention. Being healthy is as much a byproduct of biology and physicality as it is of intentional living. We maintain our body endurance by eating well and exercising. We build mental endurance by staying in a proactive perceptual state of mind.

VII. Finding Purpose
and Working Hard

"Purpose is being passionate and working hard for something that you believe matters. Success is when you look back and the memories you've made make you smile."

What fuels your passion and gives you a sense of purpose? Purpose and passion can be daunting concepts, until you simplify them. Too often these concepts are weighted with unmeetable expectations and described in words of unachievable perfection. The truth is there's no perfect definition for "purpose" and no measurement to quantify when a feeling becomes a "passion." Purpose is not an all-inclusive final answer to a life's mission, but rather a living process. It is the force driving action. Passion is the emotion connecting meaning to action. Life is filled with many purposes and many passions to fuel them!

Story 1

The Builder

— LK

A wealthy businessman had become stressed and anxious in his work. He found that he rarely left his desk, spent most of his time looking at his computer screen, didn't move much, and had little human interaction. He made a lot of money, but the pressure had affected his sleep and he became more stressed each day. He'd tried many remedies, but none worked or helped him to relax.

He found that the more tired he was, the more unable to focus he became, and the more often he looked out his window.

A new building was being built across the way. The businessman became fascinated with the process. Each day, he watched the construction workers work their bodies tirelessly lifting, pulling, hammering, drilling, soldering and doing other exhausting physical labors in all sorts of weather. The businessman quietly congratulated himself on his protected success. He thought to himself, I am fortunate to work in my luxurious office, out of the elements, and relaxing comfortably in a soft chair and warm office. They have to work no matter how they feel, for long hours, even if the weather is disagreeable. I am lucky indeed, and yet he knew that honesty would force him to admit he was not actually happy.

The businessman realized that watching the builders seemed to be the only thing he had found to relax him. He decided it would be beneficial to have one of the builders come to work in person in his office. The next day, he approached a worker and made him a very generous offer. He would pay the builder two times whatever the man made in a day to come and work for half the time in the businessman's office. The builder was over the moon with his good luck and accepted the offer immediately.

The first day, the builder came to the businessman's office he asked what he should work on to build. The businessman sat at his computer and said, "Oh, no. I do not need anything built, I just find it calming to watch you and your fellow construction workers doing the physical labor required to build. All you have to do is pretend to do your work. There is no need to exhaust yourself or risk injury, just *act* as though you are lifting, hammering, soldering, whatever it is you do." It seemed strange to the builder, but he was again stunned at this good opportunity. Not only did he get home earlier, make double the money but now his back wouldn't hurt, and his shoulder injury wouldn't flare up. The builder whistled and pretended to build . . . nothing.

After a few hours the businessman said, "That is enough for today, thank you. I feel remarkably calmer. Same time tomorrow?"

The worker was thrilled and agreed. This continued for a few days, the builder felt fortunate and the businessman calmer but by week's end the construction worker missed doing the actual work of building something. The builder told the businessman he was returning to his previous job and thanked him for the generous opportunity. The businessman tripled his offer and lessened the hours. The builder couldn't refuse. He returned the next day to perform.

The builder had become depressed and no longer looked forward to going to work. He dragged himself to the businessman's office and started to act, but then he stopped. He stared out the window across to the real building being built and told the businessman that he couldn't do it. The builder explained that there was no purpose in his work, and he needed to be part of building something real, work with other people to come together in creating something bigger than them. The worker gave the money back and returned to his old job.

The businessman finally understood. The lesson was life changing. He realized that everyone needs purpose in his/her work and to work with others in some direct or indirect way to build something bigger than themselves. It could be constructing a building, a family, a meaningful career, being part of a cause, working in or with nature or even a hobby . . . but it must have meaning. The businessman changed how he lived after that conversation. He spent more time with his family and created an organization that helped the local community. Suddenly he enjoyed his work again. In appreciation he gave a large financial gift to the builder and his family to thank him for imparting such a valuable lesson.

Thought:

The path to fulfillment cannot be bought or bypassed it must be paved with meaningful contribution to get to where you want to be. When our efforts are in alignment with our values and desires, we experience a sense of purpose in what we are doing. We associate meaning to our actions and commitments. Working to "earn" reward or progress brings substance to the experience and creates a necessary sense of purpose in how we are living our lives.

Inquiry:

1. How do you define purpose?
2. Do you feel that you have purpose in your life? In your work?
3. Is most of your time spent working in ways that contribute to what matters most to you?
4. Why do you work? What are you working for?
5. Are there ways that you can bring more meaning to your work? How?
6. Are you purposeful with how you spend your time and energy in socially?

Story 2

The Lazy Man's Load

Told with an old adage in mind.

My son was about ten years old and it was his turn to clear the table of plates after dinner. Obstinate, he began to pile the plates on top of each other. Then he reached for forks, napkins and a ketchup bottle and piled those on top of the wobbly stack of dirty dishes. His arms quivered from the bulk of the pile and yet he proceeded to grab a couple of glasses with his "free" hand. before I could speak a warning the entire stack of plates, food and ketchup had fallen to the floor.

I pulled out the garbage and set my son forward to clean up the huge mess he had created. He was really unhappy and began to complain louder, demanding help. I explained that his grandma would have called his technique the "lazy man's load" and lectured how that approach "never works out well in the long run." As my son was learning . . . taking short-cuts and choosing the lazy approach in an effort to reduce effort usually does not get a job done well and often comes back to bite you.

Thought:

Temptation stalks us through life, luring us toward "the easy way." Very often, the easy route is not the wisest or most efficient route. Though there can be benefit in streamlining effort to achieve a result, the lazy detour usually is not chosen for its wisdom but is picked as avoidance and leads to less efficient, and sometimes sloppy, outcomes.

Inquiry:

1. How do you define lazy? Would you consider yourself to be lazy often?

2. What does being efficient mean to you? Are you as efficient as you would like to be?

3. Do you often take short cuts? What is the intention behind a short cut? What are you intending to avoid?

4. When is a short cut considered to be successful?

5. Do you feel that shortcuts usually result in unfinished pieces being left behind?

6. Do you see yourself as taking the *lazy man's load* in life sometimes? Often? Why or why not?

Story 3

The Cafeteria of Life

A story told to me.

An older gentleman, new to America, had gone into a cafeteria to get something to eat. There, he sat down at an empty table and waited for someone to take his order. Of course nobody did. Finally, a woman with a tray full of food sat down opposite him and informed him how a cafeteria worked.

"Start out at that end," she pointed. "Then follow the line and pick out what you want. At the other end they'll tell you how much you have to pay."

In that experience the man later realized that he had learned how things worked in America. The gentleman explained that he viewed life in America like getting lunch at a cafeteria. You can get anything you want, as long as you are willing to pay the price. You can get success, but you'll never get it if you wait for someone to bring it to you. You have to get up and get it yourself.

Thought:

You must be willing to work for that which you desire to have. Nobody will deliver your life to you. Life is the accumulations of moments lived. Only you can put on your tray that which you want to have at the end of the line. Don't be shy about filling your tray.

Inquiry:

1. Do you find that you wait for life to deliver you opportunity?

2. If you decided to get up and serve yourself, what would be on your life tray that is not today?

3. Are you clear on what you really want? What will it take to get what you want?

4. What is the cost of getting all that you want? What is the cost of not getting it?

5. What would happen if you stopped waiting and went for everything you wanted right now?

6. What would you go for first if you didn't need permission?

Story 4

Walking the Dog

— LK

A young boy was in a store on his phone. The store manager was behind the counter listening to the young boy trying to convince someone to allow him to walk their dog for a price. The manager could tell that the woman continued to refuse the boy's offer, but the boy kept at it.

The boy asked the woman how much she paid her current dog walker and offered to charge less but the woman continued to say she was pleased with her current service. Finally, the boy relented. "I'm glad you are happy, Ma'am. I will call again to check to see if you change your mind."

The boy then went to pay for his items. The manager was so impressed with the young boy's tenacity he felt he had to say something. "I'm sorry you didn't get your job, but I heard you on the phone and you sound like a hard worker to me. I would like to offer you a job here."

The boy thanked the manager but refused because he was already was very busy and couldn't add more business to his day. The manager was confused. He asked the boy, "Why were you pursuing the woman to walk her dog so fervently if you didn't have more time for work?"

The boy smiled and said, "That lady is already my customer. I wanted to make sure she was happy, and no one could undercut my price to take away her business."

Thought:

Pride in working hard and doing a good job creates long term success. Even if one job doesn't work out, another one will if you work hard and care about your work quality. Inviting assessment of your work from your customers or even co-workers will provide data that helps you to continue to improve and grow. Take pride in what you do in life, master your efforts and stay open to feedback.

Inquiry:

1. Can you identify an area of personal mastery?

2. What special value, knowledge, or effort do you provide?

3. What would you like to be more knowledgeable about?

4. Do you check with those affected or benefiting from your work to gauge how well you are doing?

5. Do you regularly check for feedback in your relationships to gauge your part?

6. Do you assign great value to a job well done?

Summary:

Find purpose through hard work and meaningful contribution! Finding purpose and working hard gives us a sense of personal power in our own life and develops meaning through our actions. If you spend your life waiting for opportunity to come to you, or waste your time doing things for the wrong reasons or take the easy out instead of investing in your life with full energy, attention, and integrity, the results are of your own creation will likely leave large empty spaces where happiness does not thrive.

VIII. Live Empowered

"The way get started is to quit talking and begin doing."

— Walt Disney

What are you creating each day? Do you start each day refueled for a new beginning and excited to create? If not, now is the time to start. Life can be shifted, tweaked, re-written or edited to reflect more of what you want at any time. Perhaps think of one thing you want and then decide now to *go for it*! Be excited by the possibilities you envision and allow that energy to generate the power to motivate you forward. Each moment offers a new chance to do something you want to do. How will you choose to answer the invitation? Living an empowered life is putting your desires into action and creating what you want.

LAURA KITCH

Story 1

Shadows on the Wall

Summary of the allegory of Plato's cave.

In *The Republic*, Plato writes a dialogue between his brother, Glaucon, and Socrates. In the piece Socrates describes a story of a group of people who have been chained to a wall in a cave all of their lives. The entire group is stuck facing the blank wall upon which shadows dance. The prisoners don't know of the true events occurring to cause these images on the wall before them. They know nothing else but these images and watch them each day and even give them names and stories.

One day, one of the prisoners escapes the chains and sees the reality occurring behind the prisoners. The shadows the prisoners watch are projections of a real life occurring out of their sight or knowledge. There is a large fire between the prisoners and the outside of the cave where people pass, their shadows projected onto the cave wall. The prisoners still watch and see them as real. The escaped prisoner realizes the true reality and sees that the shadows are not it. He offers to free the others (as does the philosopher free humans from their delusions) but none of the other inmates desire to leave because it is the only world and truth they have ever known. This parallels the dilemma of the human condition, which is forever bound to the impressions that are received through the senses.

One day, the prisoners do manage to break free of their bonds and see the fantastical reality that had been playing behind them all along. They realize all they had thought to be real was not. Plato uses this story to emphasize the importance of education (learning of new information) and point out that it is the nature of humans to not to see the source of truth but instead to be restricted by the narrow explanations we think of as truth and knowing. We must understand that our interpretations are limited, and the truth is not yet fully seen or know but is available.

Thought:

To continue to learn we must always be pursuing new information and perspectives. We must remember that we are only seeing only a piece of a larger truth. The stories we tell ourselves are a limited version of reality and if we stay curious, we can see other parts we neglected to perceive before. The shadows we watch and the stories we create are of our own making.

Inquiry:

1. Is simplification a form of close-mindedness?

2. Can you see ways that you stay limited in your thinking? How does it serve you? How might it harm or restrain you?

3. How uncomfortable is it to accept that some of how you decided life "is", could be wrong?

4. Do you believe that a person is able to grow and learn if they stay in the same line of thinking that they have always had? How curious are you?

5. What are some of the misperceptions (shadows) you once saw as real but now see differently?

6. What have you discovered about yourself or life on your own journey that surprised or even shocked you?

Story 2

The Gambler's Debt

Anonymous.

Once there was a shady club/casino owner. He was known to partake in illegal gambling and other sorts of criminal activity, but he was never caught because he was clever. It so happened that an older man had succumbed to his tendencies for gambling and in a terrible failed evening of betting with this club owner, the man had lost all of his life savings, including his home to the club owner.

When the gambler's daughter found out about this, she stomped right down to meet with the sneaky club owner and tried to reason with him. The club owner fancied this young lady and wanted her to work in his club and as his personal assistant to pay back her father's debt. This was a horrible thought to the daughter who knew how she would be treated and held to serve this nasty man's wants. The daughter flat out refused. The club owner responded, "Well then, I am afraid that I cannot help what will happen next. If your father does not pay me, bad things do happen."

The father and the daughter were horrified by either result. The casino owner offered a bet to the daughter. Taking off his hat he turned it over to show it was empty inside and then he put a red and a black betting chip off the card table they sat at into the hat. "If you pick the red chip you must be my server and personal attendant until your father's debt is fully paid. If you choose the black chip your father's debt will be forgiven and you are free."

It seemed the only choice. The tension rose. The father and daughter were ready to weep at the thought of what could happen. The daughter was very astute and watched the sneaky owner each step as he positioned the hat toward her. She noticed that the cheating owner had sneakily removed the black chip and dropped in its place another red chip as he covered the hat and pushed the hat toward the daughter for her retrieval. They readied for her pick. The daughter felt such dread she could barely breathe. Of course, the cheating man had guaranteed she would pick a red chip and loose her bet and have to be his assistant. If she questioned the owner, he would be angry and defend his false integrity by taking it out on her father. There was no way she could win!

The question is, what would you have done if you were the daughter? If you had to advise her, what would you have told her? Logic might produce three possibilities:

1. The daughter should refuse to take a chip.
2. The daughter should expose the owner as a cheat by showing that there were two red chips in the hat.
3. The daughter should pick a red chip and sacrifice herself in order to save her father from danger.

What answer did you derive to be the best choice? The smart daughter was very wise indeed. She was quick to think up her plan. She put her hand into the hat and drew out a betting chip. Without looking at it, she fumbled and let it fall. It fell right into the pocket off the table that held a pile of black and red chips mixed together. "Oh, how clumsy of me," she said. "But never mind, if you look into the hat for the one that is left, you will be able to tell which color chip I picked."

Since the remaining chip is red, it must be assumed that she had picked the black one. And since the business owner dared not admit his dishonesty, the daughter changed what seemed an impossible situation into an advantageous one.

Thought:

Sometimes finding the solution requires examining a situation from a different viewpoint. Flexibility of approach will allow for rearrangement of information and shape new solutions. Think outside of the hat!

Inquiry:

1. How able are you to use alternative ways of thinking? Is that challenging for you?

2. Do you find you usually do things the same way each time? How could switching it up bring value?

3. Are you quick to come up with solutions?

4. How does that help or hurt you in life?

5. Do you come up with your answers before considering the other ways of looking at the issue?

6. Can you become a more flexible solution finder?

Story 3

The Seven Wonders
of the World

Author unknown.

An elementary class teacher was teaching history to her class. She handed out a surprise quiz at the end of their day with a single question on the paper . . . List Seven Wonders of the World. The teacher had covered a great many in class and was willing to accept a variety of answers. When time was up the teacher collected the papers. Most of the papers had similar answers listed. The most common answers were based on what they had studied. They were the following:

1. The Great Pyramids of Giza, Egypt
2. The Great Wall of China
3. The Colosseum, Italy
4. The Grand Canyon, United States
5. The Great Barrier Reef, Australia
6. Amazon Rainforest, Brazil
7. Hoover Dam, United States

Most of the children seemed to easily choose their answers and had been done promptly with their quizzes, but one young student seemed to be struggling. The teacher came over and asked if the student needed any help. The student looked up still considering what to put down and said, "I put down the first five, but the last two are so hard to choose. I will just pick two and be done."

The student's seven wonders of the world were:

1. To see
2. To smell
3. To touch
4. To hear
5. To taste
6. To love
7. To laugh

Isn't life and appreciation all about how we perceive it!

Thought:

Often we are reaching for the big finale rather enjoying the wonderful sensations of the experience. It is true there are great places in our world to visit, momentous occasions to celebrate and pleasures to experience but they all are nothing without the senses that convey the impressions to our minds. The sublime of the adventure lies within us all the time. We are equipped to explore the wonders of the world each day!

Inquiry:

1. How surprising was the student's list to you?

2. Do you find pleasure in the experience or often get lost in the "to-do's" and "get-to's"?

3. Do you find that you often pay attention and experience through all of your senses?

4. Think of a special experience and see how many sensory details you can remember. Did you focus on one or two senses at most? Try to imagine something in that experience through the other senses (smell, taste, . . .).

5. What brings you wonder? How do you sense wonder in your body?

6. What would your Seven Wonders of the World be?

Story 4

Find Your Sunspot

— *LK*

The shelter said Jack was a black lab . . . mix. They underplayed the mix part. Jack is definitely first part hound dog, perhaps second part lab. The hound dog in him is most noticeable in his inclination toward smell. To put it lightly, Jack follows his nose. It is possible that a scent could lead him right off of a cliff if it was appealing enough. Second to appreciating a good scent, Jack loves to run and bark. Those three activities can consume Jack in blinding participation. In the case of barking, he has a hound dog woof that could penetrate brick and though Jack loves his barking, my neighbor Patty does not. And so, I am careful not to let Jack over-indulge in his barking solos when he is outside.

On this particular day Jack was minding his yard, as he usually does. The barking began when a parade of delivery trucks came through the neighborhood one after the next. Quite quickly I realized the barking limit had been met for Patty's patience so I went to the front door to call Jack inside. I paused at the glass door to watch when I saw Jack sprinting across the lawn. Pure enjoyment infused his every inch. I smiled as this beautiful creature ran with full power and unleashed strength (all the while his pink tongue flapped out from the side of his mouth, dangling in goofy bliss.) Jack was completely consumed by his joy. Dedicated to the extended stride with every ounce of his body. His legs were spread long from front to back in a wide, reaching pace, his muscles were taut along his sides filled with adrenaline, flexing from hard work, and his black fur shined in the sunlight. I admired how present he was in his pleasure.

But then there was Patty. I waited for jack to finish his running and when he settled into a standing bark I yelled for him to come inside. I fully expected resistance. It was beautiful outside, and he was clearly enjoying it. Instead, what happened was Jack bounced his way right to the front door, into the house, and after a short acknowledgement of me with his wet nose, went into the den. With his purpose outside complete, Jack was ready to move on.

I closed the front door and followed him into the den where I saw him walk in circles and settle down on the carpet where a circle of sunlight had warmed the floor. Within seconds he was snoring. Just as committed to his relaxation as he had moments before been committed to action. Jack had found his sunspot and happily moved into a deep, satisfying sleep.

Thought:

Receive Presence. Resisting the natural progression of time creates friction. When we hold on to past experience, or reach for the next moment we imagine, we sacrifice the actual moment of living. Every event has its time and when that time has come for it to be complete, it is best to let it be and move on. Too often we "work at" being present instead of letting go to receive presence. If we expect less and receive more, we are able to appreciate the available sunspots in each moment of our living.

Inquiry:

1. Do you find that you are often consumed in thoughts about the past or worries regarding the future rather than focusing on the current moment?

2. How do you commit fully to the moment you are in when it is important to you?

3. Do you use breathing or centering techniques to help with your awareness?

4. Are you able to "let go" of disrupting thinking when you decide to?

5. Do you see how holding on to an already-lived moment or a moment that-hasn't-happened-yet could deplete being fully committed to the present experience?

6. How could you live more fully in the present?

Summary:

Live empowered! Live fully right now in the moment you have, using the senses of your body and mind to ingest and marvel at your experiences. Being confident is learning to trust your abilities and know you will get you through the challenges you face, while embracing your curiosity to lead you forward into discovery. Creating the foundation that provides love, safety and support through our commitments enables us to fly into the open blue sky of our adventures without becoming lost. We honor that which is most meaningful in our lives and use those connections to guide us as we challenge our imagination, leave our comfort zones, and explore the vast unknown of our potential. We grow and learn by stretching our wings, reaching for our possibilities and *soaring*!

Stories are our gifts to each other

This book is filled with gifts. Each story opens an opportunity for connection and exploration. Sharing our stories brings us closer together and opens our minds and hearts to other's experiences. Stories entertain us, educate us, connect us, and they reflect our humanity throughout time. Giving a story as an actual gift is powerful! This last story, "The Gift of the Raspberry," is wrapped inside of a personal experience. A story within a story. I hope it inspires you to share stories as gifts.

The Gift of the Raspberry

Unknown author.

A yoga student gave me a special gift one morning. She came in to class with a lovely gift bag and handed it to me. Inside was a scroll with a ribbon tied around it. She asked me to unroll it and explained that the paper had a story printed on it regarding Buddhism and the significance of mental workings on our physical body. An adaptation of the story is below.

*

Kate had a serious surgery that left her physically and mentally drained. For a long while she was not physically able to do much but worse than that, she was depressed and had no inclination to move herself. Her husband and her friends urged Kate to get up for at least short durations, but she would just turn over and stay in bed.

Finally, after steady persistence from her husband, Kate agreed to go for a short walk out in her back yard. When she opened the door, everything looked grey. She forced herself forward. As she stepped on the ground the leaves crackled under her feet. Everything was bare. Only sticks remained on the bushes and trees surrounding the yard. Clouds covered any sunshine and hidden color. The sky was grey and so was she. Kate was depressed and looking around this stark environment made her feel even worse. The cold bit her skin and chilled her spine but she convinced herself to walk one time around the yard before going back in to her bed.

As she walked along the perimeter of the yard the empty branches and colorless world made her feel deeply sad. Then she stopped. Something caught her attention. In one area, she spotted something blush-red inside the tangled branches. Upon closer look she noticed it was a raspberry.

Kate marveled at how the single berry had come to be ripe at this time when all the other berries were gone. She thought about all the forces of nature that brought forth this lone little raspberry that seemed so cheerful and alive. She pulled the fruit off the branch and plunked it into her mouth. Biting down on the raspberry, sugary juice filled her mouth. The sweet taste awakened her senses, as though life was being poured into her again.

She began to feel energy return as she walked toward the house with a smile across her mouth. The sweet taste lingered, and Kate felt able to make herself a cup of tea when she went back inside. She was still so surprised by the single sweet berry that she went to tell her husband about it but he was busy so she did some chores and waited for him to finish his call. When her husband came out, Kate described with an animated excitement all about the sweet fruit she had found outside. She looked out the window to the winter branches as she spoke to her husband, still surprised that a single raspberry could have thrived in the sparse environment it was in.

Days later Kate spoke to a friend, telling her about this raspberry that had affected her so deeply. Kate said she continued to think of that berry and wondered how it could have made such a difference in her. She had found renewed energy and was now up and doing many of her regular tasks.

Kate said that the sugary taste of the single surviving berry had given her the resilience to find the sweetness in her own day and move with confidence in her own strength to persevere. Seeing it persist against all of the elements reminded her that she could also thrive through her conditions.

*

I read the story from my yoga friend and loved it. On the bottom of the copy of the story my fellow yogi had written me a note. "Thank you for being a raspberry in my life."

I felt so good inside. The story and her note were hugely impactful but there was still more…at the bottom of the gift bag was a box of fresh raspberries. How incredibly simple and amazing! A note, a story, and a simple grocery store box of raspberries made me feel incredible. My friend had passed on more than a story, she had given me the gift of appreciation and connection. All of us want to feel that what we offer to the world and to other people "matters". Connection creates meaning in our lives and acknowledgement makes people feel valued. What could be a better gift to someone you care about?

I have not stopped feeling the effects of her gift. The caring touch of appreciation in a simple but complete gesture. It has stayed with me as inspiration to this day, many years later, and attached to that memory is a warm feeling that I now try to remember to spread. It has become the virtual sweetness that often inspires me to push through my own difficult times.

I asked my friend for permission to share the story of her gift and invite copycats in the yoga classes I taught. She was happy to share the idea of making a positive difference in other's lives. Since then, many have heard about the gift of "The Gift of the Raspberry" and given the story away to people important to them. Some gave just the story, some gave the raspberries too, but we all extended the reach of appreciation to someone special in our lives.

My full gratitude goes to all in our ever-growing community of story sharers. Let's keep connecting exponentially!

Remember . . .

Know who you are

Explore what you believe

Be responsible for your choices

Build support for what you want and need

Trust yourself

Maintain a positive attitude

Work hard and with purpose

Live powerfully!

About the Author

Laura Kitch lives in New York with her family. She is a mom, yoga teacher, motivational speaker, freelancer writer, and author. She is the owner of MindfulCalm, a Yoga and Life Coaching Agency where she teaches yoga and holds motivational workshops and trainings as well as continues to work with individual clients. Laura is passionate about sharing stories and is excited to share the newly released, *Black Dog Zen* motivational story guides for adults, beginning with *Volume 1: Finding Your Sunspot.* She hopes these stories strengthen our connections and inspire us to reach toward each other with curiosity and compassion.

Connect with Laura on Facebook, Instagram, or Twitter.

Made in the USA
Middletown, DE
09 December 2021

54714790R00116